DIN   ASA
‾‾‾‾‾‾‾‾
·15 — 25
19 — 64
21 — 100
23 — 160
24 — 200
26 — 320
27 — 400
30 — 800

Theo Kisselbach
LEICA CL

A

Theo Kisselbach

LEICA CL

English Edition by
E. F. Linssen, FZS, FRES, FRPS.

HOVE CAMERA FOTO BOOKS

FIRST GERMAN EDITION
1976

FIRST ENGLISH EDITION
May 1977

ISBN 0 85242 570 8

Published in English by
HOVE CAMERA FOTO BOOKS
34 Church Road,
Hove, East Sussex,
United Kingdom.

Originally published in German by Heering-Verlag Gmbh, Seebruck am Chiemsee
Western Germany.

© Heering-Verlag Gmbh & Hove Camera Foto Books.

Printed by Design & Print, Shoreham-by-Sea, West Sussex, United Kingdom.

CONTENTS

5

Why compact?

A camera which is small, and light, like the first model 50 years ago — that has been, and still is the wish of many Leica devotees. Leitz have now fulfilled that wish. In order to achieve a really pocket size camera, the focal plane shutter has been redesigned and in this new camera travels down the shorter format dimension, from top to bottom. The shutter release is extremely quiet, the shutter running smoothly and softly. These are necessary conditions for freedom from camera shake, permitting full use of the lens performance.

The new camera is not intended to replace the Leica M5. It was deliberately based on a different conception. Statistic analysis has shown that for almost 90% of the photographs taken by Leica photographers lenses of between 28 and 90 mm are used, and from this it clearly follows that for many photographs a shorter rangefinder base should suffice. Any such shortening necessarily effects a considerable saving of space.

The Leica CL serves a twofold purpose: as an independent compact camera, and as a supplement to the Leica system. Notwithstanding its small overall size, it covers the full 24 x 36 mm format. This guarantees quality, even in colour photography, and for no other format is so wide a range of films available.

Two special lenses have been developed for this camera: the Leitz Summicron-C f/2, 40 mm, as a universal lens of high light transmission and wide angle, and the Leitz Elmar-C f/4, 90 mm as a handy telephoto lens. The Leica CL has the same bayonet lens interchange as the M-Leicas, enabling many Leica lenses to be used with it.

The exposure problem has been very neatly solved. In similar fashion to the Leica M5, the light intensity is measured from behind the lens by a CdS photoresistor which swings in a few millimetres in front of the focal plane shutter. On pressing the release the photocell springs out from the light path before the shutter begins to move. It measures only a small area of the image in the centre of the field. The diameter of the measuring surface of the CdS photoresistor is 7.5 mm. which for a 90 mm focal length corresponds approximately to that of the rangefinder measuring area in the viewfinder.

There is no automatic exposure determination in this camera: each subject can be individually measured and set on the controls, free choice of stop and shutter speed being an important factor in photographic composition.

The Leica CL is handy and quick to operate. With its very small weight it is scarcely any encumbrance, and can therefore be carried around everywhere.

But to make the best use of it, we need to be fully aware of its potentialities, and equally of its limitations.

To concentrate so much technology into so small a space is possible only with a rangefinder camera. With such a camera the scene is viewed through a miniature optical system located above and beside the camera lens. At very short working distances, the fact that the viewfinder axis is displaced relatively to the camera axis (parallax) can present difficulties. For this reason the minimum working distance has been limited to 0.8 metre.

A single-lens reflex camera has no such parallax. The image which appears on its focusing screen is actually projected, via a mirror, by the camera lens itself. In order to expose the film, the mirror has to be swung out of the light path, and that needs space, which increases the minimum distance between the lens bayonet and the film, which in turn demands, in the case of wide angle camera lenses, the employment of expensive "retrofocus" types. The prism system, too, which is needed to correct the lateral reversal of the finder image, calls for yet more space. All these factors contribute to the extra size and weight inherent in the single-lens system, it is therefore understandable that the rangefinder system should have been adopted for the Leica CL.

Focusing with a rangefinder is rapid and effective. The luminous reflected frames indicate the format coverage for 40, 50, and 90 mm lenses, and in the case of the 50 and 90 mm lenses the finder field covers also the immediate environment outside the actual picture area, which is a great advantage in street scenes and sports photography. There is no interruption of continuous viewing of the scene through the finder, as happens with the single-lens reflex, the subject still remaining in view at the actual instant of exposure. Thus it is possible to repeat, say, a portrait if it should happen that the subject chose just that instant to blink. In the case of flash exposures, also, any disturbing reflections become apparent.

In the following pages will be found much information, with many examples, on the details of photographic technique in general, and in particular on the functioning and performance of the Leica CL.

A series of sectional diagrams will clarify, for those technically interested, the interaction of the individual components, and clearly illustrate what is meant by compact construction.

Remember that experience is as essential as instructions. The more photography you practise, the more familiar will the operation of the Leica CL become. It will then not be long before you take it everywhere with you — without the least inconvenience — because it is inconspicuous, light in weight, and always ready for use.

Seeing photographically

There is, however, one important feature of photography, and that is that it records every detail in the subject quite regardless of whether it is, or is not, actually wanted.

Still more important is another feature which is best explained by examples. A doorway is about two metres high. Viewed from a distance of 2.5 metres it does not look twice as big as when viewed from 5 metres distance. A head viewed from 1 metre does not look three times as big as from 3 metres. This automatic visual adaptation is a vitally important phenomenon. In photography, on the other hand, the image size follows .the laws of central projection, and takes full account of the working distance. Unless we are fully aware of the implications of this situation, we may very easily fall into the error of making inadequate use of the image format.

Photography constitutes our most efficient aide-memoire. Our memory is limited in its capacity, and needs assistance. But not everything which we see with our eyes can be photographically recorded in just the same form. The eye and the camera each have their own way of recording, and if we are to take good photographs we must learn to "see photographically".

Two things are important in photography. The first is the technical process, which is dependent upon the equipment. The second, and more important, is our approach. We must consider carefully what it is we want. Nearly all these questions begin with a "W": What? Where? When?, Who? Whither? What with? .... and .. How?

How to use the Leica CL is a matter of studying the instructions. It is not enough just to skim through them. Better to follow this rule: Practise every operation until you can perform it automatically. As with driving a car: it is safe to drive only when clutch, gear change, and braking have become automatic. Specially important is to practise loading the camera and winding on the film. In order that the exercise may correspond to normal practice, a waste film can be used which cannot be used for actual photography.

After a little practice, everything will go perfectly, even if we are in a hurry. Nevertheless there is one fault which frequently occurs with beginners. Since it happens to young and old alike, regardless of how experience has been achieved, its cause must lie outside the purely photographic aspect. If we consider the behaviour of the human eye we can find the explanation.

It is very little trouble to carry around with you an empty slide mount and, when the occasion demands, hold it up to your eye as a viewing frame. You will be surprised how quickly this will teach you to see pictorially.

The eye and the camera

In many text books the camera is likened to the eye, because some functions are common to both. True, the eye has a lens and a layer sensitive to light. But our vision becomes effective only through the action of the brain, which has to make many corrections. The image on the retina of the eye is upside down, yet we see everything the right way up. If we move our head, or eyes, we see no movement of our environment. Similarly when we ourselves are in motion. Yet if something in that environment does actually move, we are aware of it.

The field of view of the eye, both horizontally and vertically, is very great, but it is only a very small area which we see clearly. We scan the visible field for objects of interest, but the brain registers only such details as we consider important.

So we must learn to see photographically, there is one outstanding short cut to this end. If we close one eye and hold the empty (5 x 5 cm) frame of a slide mount at a match stick distance (5 cm) from the other, what we see through it corresponds to the field of view of a normal focus lens, and consequently to the image in the camera viewfinder. If we wish to photograph some object so as to fill the format, we must approach it sufficiently closely as to do just this with our slide mount, leaving no empty space around our subject.

The distance of the mount from the eye must be the same as the focal length of the lens to be used. Thus if we reduce it to 40 mm, we shall see the field as covered by a 40 mm lens; if we lengthen it to 90 mm, the field will change to that of a 90 mm lens. Thus composition becomes easier with the longer focal lengths: there is less in the picture, the important detail becomes larger, and more significant within the field.

Confidence in camera manipulation

For good photography, it is absolutely essential so completely to master the details of camera manipulation that it becomes automatic, leaving us free to devote our attention wholly and completely to composition. The same sequence of operations should always be adhered to:

1. Set stop and shutter speed (whether the stop or the shutter speed is to be the primary consideration will depend upon the nature of the subject and the exposure conditions).

2. Adjust focus or set to distance.

3. Press the release.

Since every exposure necessitates pressing the release, this procedure is of special importance. The utmost care must be taken that the pressing of the release does not move or tilt the camera. Check your release techniques in front of a mirror — of course with no film in the camera! The longer the focal length of the lens, the greater is the risk of movement blur.

Getting to know how a camera functions is a twofold exercise: first we must use our brains to understand its mechanical operation, and then learn to use our hands to control it. The more often we practise the individual operations, the sooner we shall reach the stage when we can carry them out automatically without thinking about them.

1. Automatic frame counter
2. Rapid film wind lever
3. Shutter speed scale index
4. Film speed setting knob
5. Release button
6. Shutter speed setting ring
7. Red spot index
8. Lock button for lens interchange
9. Accessory shoe with centre contact
10. Depth of field scale
11. Aperture scale
12. Distance scale
13. Rangefinder window
14. Illumination window for luminous frame
15. Viewfinder window
16. Eyes for camera sling
17. Viewfinder eyepiece
18. Rewind crank
19. Lock for camera base plate
20. Tripod socket
21. Press button for rewind release
22. Film reminder disc.

How to hold the camera

The usual procedure is to hold the camera so as to look with the right eye through the finder. The left eye can however be used if this gives better vision. Hold the camera firmly in both hands, if possible resting it against the head to give extra support. Bring the eye close enough to the finder to render the whole finder field fully visible.

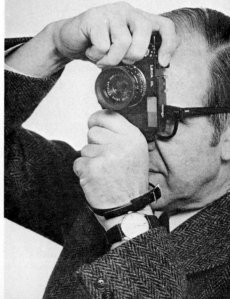

For vertical formats there are two possibilities. If you use the right eye for the finder, grasp the camera so that the tip of the right thumb rests on the release button. The alternative is to use the index finger for the release as with the horizontal format. This position is preferable if you use the left eye, since you can then support the right hand against the forehead.

The rapid wind lever has two functions. It transports the film from one frame to the next, when swung as far as it will go in the direction of the arrow. It also switches on the exposure meter when the shutter is cocked and the lever lifted slightly away from the camera body. So long as the lever rests close against the body the exposure meter remains switched off.

Shutter cocking and release

One swing of the rapid wind lever (2) as far as it will go transports the film by one frame and simultaneously cocks the shutter and automatically moves on the frame counter. The release can only be operated provided the lever has been taken right to the stop.

The release button (5) is provided with a screw thread for attachment of a cable release (Order No. 14067). Press the release slowly — not roughly — until the shutter operates. Pressure of the lever in the wind direction (when the shutter is cocked) prevents release.

The shutter speed setting ring (6) controls the shutter speed and can be set before or after cocking the shutter. It has click settings at all engraved speeds from 1/1000 to ½ sec and B (time exposures of any duration). Intermediate values are fully effective *(with the exception of those between 1/30 and 1/60 sec)*. The shutter speed scale index (3) is located on the top of the camera body. When using flash, the shutter speed setting ring should be set to 1/60 sec (engraved yellow) or a slower speed (See also flash table on page 33).

15

Lens interchange

Removal: With the right hand grasp the lens by the rear fixed ring (10) and with the thumb of the left hand press down the catch (8): rotate the lens anti-clockwise and remove it.

Insertion: The red spot on the lens mount must coincide with the red catch (8) on the camera body. When the two surfaces are in contact, turn slightly clockwise until the bayonet is heard to click into position.

In the case of short focus lenses the last lens surface is open and unprotected. Before, therefore, inserting the lens make sure that the surface is scrupulously clean. Lenses should not be changed in full light, but in the shadow of the body.

The function of the diaphragm is to control the quantity of light passing through the lens. The diaphragm stop numbers are internationally standardized. They represent the ratio of the diameter of the diaphragm to the focal length of the lens. For simplification, the numerator of the fraction is omitted, only the denominator is engraved. Thus —4 — signifies f/4.

The diaphragm scale (11) is so divided that stopping down from number to number in each case calls for a doubling of the exposure. Many lenses have click stops and half stops.

Distance and depth-of-field scales: The distance for which the focus is set can be read off from the distance scale (12). Used in conjunction with the depth-of-field scale (10) this indicates the extent of the depth of field.

Definition is acceptable between the two distances which coincide with the same stop number.

Depth of field

Strictly speaking, the only detail which is rendered perfectly sharp is that which lies in the plane upon which the lens is focused. Anything else, in front of or behind this "focused" plane, will be unsharp. However, every photographic image has a certain "depth of field", which is defined as the range in front of and behind the focused distance within which the fall-off in sharpness is still not noticeable. This range becomes shorter the closer the working distance from lens to subject. The depth of field is also dependent upon the stop used and the focal length of the lens. The smaller the stop, the greater is the depth of field, so that it becomes possible by the use of small stops, to include within the range of acceptable sharpness subject features (foreground and background) at widely differing distances. Short focus lenses have a greater depth of field than those of longer focus.

With large stops and the lens focused upon close detail the distant background will become so blurred as to cease to be a recognizable feature of the picture. In modern photography this is turned to advantage as a factor in composition.

Desirable as is a considerable depth of field, it often becomes advisable to sacrifice it. With longish exposures it increases the risk of movement blur. A compromise is thus enforced in the stopping down of the lens by the two requirements — sufficient depth of field and a sufficiently short exposure. The stops most employed are $f/4$, $f/5.6$, and $f/8$.

Unsharpness tolerance is specified by what is termed the "circle of confusion". This is the diameter, expressed as a fraction of a millimetre, of the circular spot which is formed by the out-of-focus image of a point. In the depth-of-field scales and tables published for the Leica the standard adopted is $1/30$ mm.

The influence of the stop on depth of field

If, for example, we are using the Summicron-C $f/2$, 40 mm lens, focused on 5 metres, at $f/5.6$ the depth of field extends from about 3 to 10 metres. If on the other hand we stop down to $f/11$, the depth of field will cover from about 2.5 metres to infinity.

If in the first case a shutter speed of $1/250$ sec is possible, at $f/11$ the corresponding speed is $1/60$ sec.

With longer focus lenses the depth of field is considerably narrower. This can be seen from a comparison with the Elmar-C $f/4$, 90 mm, exact details of which are given in the table on page 132.

18

Depth of field at f/4, 3.5 to 8.5 metres

Depth of field at f/8, 2.75 to 27 metres

Depth of field at f/16, 2.00 metres to infinity

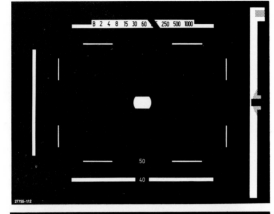

Luminous frames with 40 and 50 mm masks

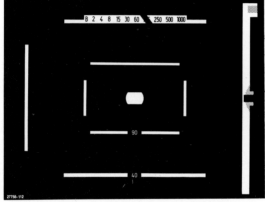

Luminous frames with 40 and 90 mm masks

The luminous frame view and rangefinder

One of the most important components of the camera is the luminous frame view and rangefinder. This simultaneously presents framing, image sharpness, and shutter speed. Since all these factors can be assessed in one and the same field, it is possible to adjust them rapidly to optimum values. This gives the Leica CL great speed of operation.

In order to understand the construction and operation of the finder, let us first cover the finder window (15) with a small opaque card. On looking through the finder we shall now see, clearly against a dark background, the luminous frames showing the framing of the respective formats. The

20

rangefinder measuring field in the centre, the shutter speed scale along the top edge, and the notch for the exposure meter needle on the right hand edge.

The luminous frames are controlled by masks placed behind the window located on the left beside the finder window. If we remove our black card, the general black area will be replaced by the viewfinder image, the other, reflected, images however remaining visible.

Luminous frames will always be visible for two focal lengths. The outside, rather wider frame for the field of the 40 mm lens does not change. Normally the 50 mm and 40 mm frames appear. If, however, we are using a 90 mm lens instead of the 50 mm, the 90 mm frame appears. The luminous frame is so coupled with the distance setting that parallax — the distance between the lens axis and finder axis — is automatically compensated. In the centre of the finder field is the measuring field of the rangefinder.

Viewfinder field with frames for 40 and 50 mm lenses. The scale at the top shows the shutter speed. The needle of the exposure meter has to be brought to the notch in the middle of the bar on the right.

Focusing

The accuracy of measurement of a range-viewfinder is dependent upon the length of the measuring base and the size of the image. The Leica CL has a base length of 31.5 mm and a viewfinder image scale of 0.6, giving an effective base length of 19 mm. This is quite adequate for the Compact lenses, but for some Leica lenses there are limitations. In the chapter "Compatibility with the Leica system", page 56, precise details are given, which should be borne in mind.

The measuring field of the rangefinder can be seen as a bright area in the middle of the field. When the focus is set to infinity (00) any object at a nearer distance is seen as a double image. As the focusing ring of the lens is rotated these two images come together and finally coalesce into a single image (coincidence method).

Still more exact is the following method, in which the subject feature viewed is a line which cuts the long edge of the measuring field (see illustration), i.e. extends beyond the limits of the measuring field. As before, the two images of the line are brought into coincidence by rotating the focusing ring (split image method).

For distances closer than 2 metres using vertical format the following technique has proved useful: a suitable distance is set in advance on the lens focusing control. Looking through the viewfinder the photographer moves backwards or forwards until the images in the measuring field coalesce. This is particularly to be recommended for portraits with the 90 mm lens.

For ametropic users who do not wear spectacles, correction lenses can be inserted in the rangefinder eyepiece (17). The Order No. 14081 must be accompanied by the dioptric correction value. These lenses are available from 0.5 — 3 dioptres, plus and minus.

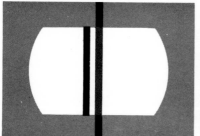

Broken line = unsharp   *Continuous line* = sharp

Setting the film speed

The first essential for correct exposure is the exact setting of the film speed. This is done by means of the knob (4) which is located on the front of the shutter speed setting ring (6). The setting knob has two windows, on opposite sides, one showing the DIN and the other the ASA speed value. The knob has to be pressed down and rotated to left or right until the desired speed number appears in the window. In the centre of the outer edge of the window is a small notch, which indicates the exact setting position. The range of speeds provided for is from 15 to 33 DIN (25 — 1600 ASA). Intermediate values can be set.

In the case of black-and-white films the effective speed can be modified by control of development.

The exposure meter

The exposure meter comes into action only when the shutter is wound and the rapid wind lever (2) is lifted away from the camera body by about 1 cm (see illustration page 23, top right). If the lever is pressed back against the body the exposure meter switches off.

Measurement is made through the camera lens on the principle of selective measurement of the central area. This receptive area comprises a CdS photoresistor 7.5 mm in diameter which while in use is located 8 mm in front of the film plane. The cell swings out from the light path immediately before the exposure and returns to its operating position when the shutter is rewound.

In making the measurement, the measurement area is sighted on an important feature of the subject. Extended to the complete circle it corresponds to the measuring area of a 90 mm lens. If a 40 mm lens is used, the measuring area is about twice as great. Measurements should always be made with the camera in horizontal format position.

No additional area has been provided in order not to further complicate the clarity of the viewfinder field.

On the right of the viewfinder field is seen the indicator needle of the exposure meter. Exposure is correctly set when the needle appears in the central rectangular notch. To bring it into this position, we can adjust either the stop or the shutter speed. The shutter speed as set can be read off along the top edge of the viewfinder field.

Thus it is left to choose whether the stop or the shutter speed is to be the dominating factor in the exposure combination. This is important where deliberate pictorial composition is involved.

If, on setting a chosen speed on the shutter speed ring (6), a red warning sign appears on the right at the edge of the finder, the ring should be adjusted until the red sign disappears. The needle is brought to the correct position by adjusting the aperture. If this is not possible, it indicates that the prevailing light conditions are outside the measuring range.

The limiting sensitivity of the exposure meter at $f/2$ is 1 cd/m^2 (candela per square metre — the international standard of light intensity). Photographically expressed this means, for $f/2$, ½ sec for 21 DIN / 100 ASA film. At low light intensities measurement should be made at full aperture, as this increases the energy reaching the photoresistor.

There is practically no limitation at high light intensity, since the lens stop can always be adequately closed down.

DIN	15	. .	18	. .	21	.	.	24	.	.	27	.	.	30	.	.	33

ASA	25		50		100		200		400		800		1600
		32 40		64 80		125 180		250 360		500 640		1000 1250	

The engraved ASA values are printed in bold type. Intermediate values are best set on the click stops between the engraved values.

Checking and replacing batteries

The built-in CdS exposure meter operates on the photoresistor principle. The current supply source is a 1.35 volt mercury cell such as the Mallory button cell PX 625. Other makes of the same characteristics, such as the Varta Pertrix 7002 or Mallory National H-D, are equally suitable. The amount of current used is so minute that the cells usually fail in the end from sheer old age. One can reckon on a life of 1-2 years, but 3 years is not unusual.

Whether or not the cell is still giving sufficient current can be checked as follows: Hold the camera in the horizontal format position and look through the finder. Rotate the shutter speed ring until the pointer appears in the upper right-hand corner of the finder field. Press the test button (23). If the battery is still in good condition the needle will swing to the rectangular notch in the middle of the exposure meter strip.

To change the button cell the camera back must be opened. The cell lies beneath the film take-up spool (see illustration) and can easily be replaced. If, at the time, the camera is loaded, this must of course be carried out in the dark. There is no difficulty in this, since the container is so designed that the cell cannot be incorrectly inserted. After the change has been made, the battery test should be carried out to ensure that all is in order. If with a relatively new cell no current seems to be forthcoming, check the contacts for oxidation.

When taking a long trip, it is advisable to take a spare cell if the cell in the camera has already been in use for a considerable time.

Why selective measurement?

If, in exposure determination, a measurement is made of all the light which reaches the film format, this is termed integral measurement. Such an exposure determination rests on the assumption that on the average a "normal" subject reflects 17% of the light which falls upon it. This is the basis upon which exposure meters are calibrated.

However, many photographic subjects deviate from this norm. If the difference is not great, the deviation of the optimum exposure from the standard should not be significant. Even reversal colour films, which have only a small exposure latitude, will tolerate half a stop over or underexposure.

Trouble however arises with subjects which exhibit great differences of brightness. Such include very interesting subjects such as contre-jour and night shots, circus or ice shows in floodlighting, interior exposures including windows, etc., and it is such situations which call for selective measurement in determining the optimum exposure, since this system excludes from measurement the sources of error.

With this system the measurement is restricted to a limited area of the subject, so by directing the range-viewfinder image so that its area coincides with the feature of the subject for which correct exposure is of especial importance. Since the photocell is likewise calibrated for this same reflective value of 17%. It should be directed neither at a black nor a white area, but at some average tone in the subject which, as already mentioned, is one of importance to the picture. How this is applied in practice is best explained by examples. In interiors, brightness is very difficult to estimate and we are dependent wholly on our exposure meter. Nevertheless we still have to judge lighting contrasts, and likewise check whether there are any special limitations as to stop or shutter speed.

Take, for example, the requirements of the photograph in the Berlin Dahlem Sculpture Museum reproduced opposite. Photography in the museum is permitted, but tripods and flash are not. The sculptures are so exquisitely light anyway that a frontal flash illumination would be most unsuitable. For a hand-held exposure 1/30 sec, or better, even, 1/60 sec is advisable, so we must check what corresponds to this exposure time. The circle indicates the area on which the measurement was taken.

"Saint John" from the Munnerstadt Evangelist Group by Tilman Riemenschneider (1490-92). Summicron-C 40 mm, f/4, 1/60 sec, 160 ASA film.

For the winter landscape on the page opposite, the exposure measurement was not made on the sunlit snow, which would have given too short an exposure. The circle indicates an area containing some darker gradation. In the case of a snow subject which exhibits no such features, the measurement should be made on a sunlit hand.

Pokrowski sobor (St. Basil's Cathedral) with the Minin and Posharski Memorial in Moscow's Red Square (night photograph). Summicron-C f/2, 40 mm, 1/15 sec, 400 ASA film. The area selected for exposure determination is indicated by the circle.

In the lower photograph, taken in a church, the area selected for measurement is likewise indicated. In this way the disturbing effect of the chandelier has been eliminated. Summicron-C f/2, 40 mm, 1/30 sec, 400 ASA film.

Much greater difficulties are encountered in interior photography when large windows are included in the picture. Features which present no difficulty to visual observation can constitute a problem for the photographer. Where, for example, the interior as such calls for an exposure of ½ sec at f/8, for the area close to the window 1/125 sec might be correct at the same aperture, and if it is the interior detail itself which is of importance, the window areas would then be grossly overexposed. The only way in which full compensation could be achieved would be by the use of additional (flash) lighting for the window.

Thus an integral measurement, which necessarily must include the windows, would give an unsatisfactory reading. With the Leica CL, the use of selective measurement can obviate such errors, since for the measurement we can choose an area which does not border on the windows. A certain degree of light scatter around the window edge, in the presence of so high a contrast, is unavoidable.

Examples of the advantage of selective exposure measurement will be found in night photography, in circus and theatre photography, and in fact in any circumstances where the lighting is irregularly distributed. Frequently the general environment is almost completely in darkness. By sighting the exposure measurement on an important feature of the subject the correct exposure is determined without any difficulty. It will be evident, incidentally, that the measurement circle must not be too large if this method is to function effectively even in unfavourable lighting situations.

Besides the normal average subjects with gradation from white to black there are the exceptional cases, e.g. winter landscapes. Notwithstanding the great brilliance of such subjects it often happens that they are underexposed, if we fail to bear in mind that our exposure meter is calibrated for 17% average reflection, because the snow often reaches a reflection value of 80%. What, then, are we to do? Measurement is made over the area within the circle. If there is no feature of the subject which, over this area, exhibits an "average" relection, then the best way is to make the measurement on the palm of sun-illuminated hand.

There is one useful piece of advice in exposure determination: First estimate, then measure. This "pre-estimation" before measurement should develop our faculty for critically evaluating "brightness" and "contrast" which otherwise would just go to waste. If we blindly go by the meter indication we scarcely notice the errors which can occur. On the other hand they become strikingly evident when after making a few exposures we realize that we have forgotten to set the camera to the correct film speed. In the case of subjects in full sunlight, we come to remember a few "standard" values for stop and shutter speed readings with which our exposure meter repeatedly presents us.

Loading the film

With the Leica CL film loading is simple and convenient. Nevertheless there are certain points which we need to note, even though we may be familiar with the loading of other Leica models, because there are a few differences in procedure.

First of these is to check, by rotating the rewind crank (18) in the direction of the arrow, that the camera is not already loaded. If any resistance is felt, the film should be wound back as described in the next section.

Important note! Only cassettes with standard spools may be used. These have pilot pins at both ends (DIN 4535). Leitz metal cassettes cannot be used.

To open the camera, raise the lever (19) and turn it to the left, when the back of the camera can be removed downwards. It will remain attached to the camera strap. The film pressure plate is then swung away downwards leaving the film track free. The film tongue can be — it does not have to be — trimmed. Grip it (emulsion side upwards) between the thumb and forefinger of the right hand and push it from above into one of the slots of the take-up spool so that the perforated edge lies up against the flange of

By rotating the rewind lever in the direction of the arrow, check that the camera is not already loaded. If it is empty, raise the lever (19) and turn it to the left.

The entire camera back can now be withdrawn downwards and remains attached to the camera only by the carrying strap. The film pressure plate can now be swung up.

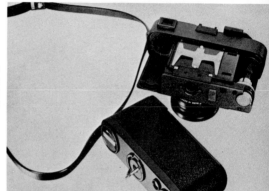

The film tongue is pushed into one of the slots obliquely from above until its perforated edge lies close against the flange of the spool.

The cassette is then carried over the open film track and placed in the cassette chamber. The film pressure plate is then closed, the camera back replaced and locked with the lever (19).

The text should be referred to for further details.

the spool. Finally lay the film over the film track and place the cassette in the space provided. The edge of the film will then lie parallel to the film guide.

Carefully operate the rapid wind lever (2) so that the teeth of the transport sprocket drum engage in perforations of the film. This can be assisted by gentle pressure with the thumb if any difficulty is encountered. Swing down the pressure plate, taking care that the sprockets are properly engaging in the perforations.

Replace the camera back and lock it with the lever (19). Give the film wind lever one turn, rotate the rewind crank (18) in the direction of the arrow until slight resistance is encountered. (This is especially important with 20-exposure cassettes).

Release the shutter. With the second turn of the film wind lever the rewind crank must be seen to rotate backwards with the film. After the third operation of the film wind lever the camera is ready for use. The frame counter (1) operates only when the camera back is properly in place and locked.

After loading the film into the camera, set the exposure meter (4) to the correct film speed, and turn the film reminder disc to the appropriate symbol. The symbols are as follows:

          ▭ = black-and-white film
          ☼ = daylight colour film
          ♀ = artificial light colour film
      NG = negative colour film

Unloading the camera

When the last frame has been exposed, the rapid wind lever will refuse to wind on, and the film must be rewound into its original cassette. First of all press the button of the rewind release (21) on the base of the camera: this frees the film transport sprocket. Swing out the rewind crank (18) and rotate it in the direction of the arrow until the film — following a slight resistance — has been completely rewound. Then open the camera as described in the fourth paragraph of the section on loading the film.

For convenience in processing, it is helpful if the film tongue is not rewound completely into the cassette. However in order to ensure that a used film will not, inadvertently, be reloaded as a new film, I make several sharp folds in the film tongue.

Flash synchronization

"Synchronization" comprises the means utilized to ensure that the flash occurs within the period that the shutter is completely open. Any type of flash unit which is provided with a centre contact attachment can be used directly with the Leica CL. The flash unit is pushed into the accessory shoe (9) and is then immediately ready for use with the appropriate shutter speeds.

Flash units with cable connection can be used only with the help of a small synchronizing adapter for pushing into the accessory shoe. Such adapters are available on the market.

Electronic flash units are all automatically triggered through an X-contact. Since the vast majority of flash bulbs today are of short flash duration, and can therefore be used with the X-contact, the Leica CL is equipped with this contact only.

The focal plane shutter runs close in front of the film. Using shutter speeds no faster than are given in the following table, the film frame remains completely open during the flash discharge, whose duration is considerably shorter than the camera shutter speed

FLASH TABLE   Electronic flash   B — 1/60 sec
               Flash bulbs M2
                            AG1
                            AG3   B — 1/30 sec
               Flash cubes (with electric triggering)

Further details concerning practical photography with flash will be found in the chapter "Flash photography", page 91.

Attaching the shoulder strap or sling

The shoulder strap and sling supplied are both attached in the same way. The shoulder pad is first slipped on to the shoulder strap, the free end of which is then passed through the two lateral eyelets (16). The strap is then pushed through the buckle and fixed at the desired length.

One or other of these straps should always be used, since when changing films it also retains hold of the camera back, which otherwise would be left lying loose.

Ever-ready case

The ever-ready case, in supple nap leather, provides an outside protection for the Leica CL. It has an easily opened zip fastener and is provided with two small holes through which the camera strap or sling can be threaded. In use, the case can be somewhat pushed back: it is so light that it is in no way an encumbrance. Since the Elmar-C f/4, 90 mm is supplied in a nap leather pouch, it provides with the ever-ready camera case a convenient combination for the two CL lenses — the 40 mm and the 90 mm.

The CL Combi case

Those who for the sake of rapid working do not wish to use an ever-ready case will use the camera on the shoulder strap, with the CL Combi case for their protection and storage. It accommodates the Leica CL with 40 mm or 90 mm lens attached, a second lens, and some films and filters. It measures 17 x 16 x 9 cm. This case will at the same time hold a small electronic flash if the 90 mm lens is mounted on the camera.

SMALL ACCESSORIES

Correction lenses

A correction lens can be inserted in the viewfinder eyepiece of the Leica CL. For spectacle wearers no further correction is needed. However there are cases of very slight visual error which do not demand the wearing of spectacles but which yet prevent adequately sharp focusing. In ordering, the ophthalmic prescription for distance should accompany the order. Only the prescription for the eye which will be used with the viewfinder is necessary. Cylindrical lenses for correction of astigmatism are not supplied, but only spherical correction lenses of +0.5, 1, 1.5, 2, and 3 dioptres, and -1, -2, and -3 dioptres.

Cable release

Cable releases should be of the type with locking screw. For long exposures the shutter can then be held open (on "Bulb") as long as desired. Cable releases are available in a variety of lengths. The 50 cm release costs only a very little more, and offers many advantages in practical use.

Small tripod and ball-and-socket head

This small, light, table tripod with three adjustable legs (Order No. 14100) can be very useful on many occasions. The small ball-and-socket head supplied to fit it (14119) permits tilting and panning of the camera. If supported against a wall, a tree, or a pillar, it provides a firm support — even for relatively long exposures, especially when used in conjunction with a cable release.

The internal technicalities of the Leica CL

The above diagrammatic picture, and the latter sectional diagrams, give an idea of the inner workings of the Leica CL. Those who are interested in details of design will find them worthy of study. Those who are less concerned with such technical details can turn to page 45, for despite the apparent complication of the diagrams the Leica CL really is quite simple in operation.

It is the same as with a car. There are quite a lot of people who would like just to drive, so far as possible in comfort, but who would also be quite interested to learn something of the reasons for details of design. Such details are no longer any secret, but just arguments for the buyer.

Designing a compact camera is no easy problem, involving as it does the accommodation, within a very limited space of a large number of components in such a way that their functioning does not interfere with anything else in the system.

The first illustration is a diagrammatic picture from which can be seen how part of the interior mechanism operates. Numbers and explanations are deliberately omitted: these are dealt with in subsequent sectional diagrams.

The diagram however also clearly shows typical features of the Leica CL;

The path of rays in the luminous frame range-viewfinder.

Selective light measurement through the lens, with swing-out photo-resistor.

Softly running focal plane shutter, running now from top downwards across the narrow dimension of the format.

The now long-standing Leica bayonet lens mount, as in the M models.

Front view of longitudinal section

This section shows a great number of interesting elements. The numbers refer to the names of the individual components or to their functions. Note that these numbers refer only to the relevant diagram.

1. Rapid film wind lever, 2. Control cams for shutter speed indication in the finder, for exposure meter, and for shutter speed escapement, 3 and 4. Shutter driving gears, 5. Control lever for slow speed escapement (22), 6. Release button, which also initiates swing-out of photoresistor, 7. Release coupling, 8. Control slider for speed indicator in viewfinder, 9. Lever to rotate meter housing, 10. Galvanometer, 11. Rangefinder roller and lever, 12. Red finder warning signal, 13. Meter needle, 14. Luminous frames, 15. Masks for selection of luminous frames for the relevant focal lengths via the slider (16), 17. Film cassette, 18. Finder window, 19. Frame counter, 20. Film transport shaft, 21. Control lever for fast shutter speeds, 22. Escape mechanism for slow shutter speeds, 23. Film spool with fixing slot, 24. Eccentric control for photoresistor, 25. Button cell (exposure meter current supply), 26 and 27. Rewind clutch, 28 and 29. Lever linkage for swinging in the photoresistor and cocking the shutter, 30. Catch for freeing the photoresistor on pressing the release button (6) via tension spring (33), 31. Camera back release, 32. Photoresistor (cadmium sulphide cell), 33. Spring for swinging out the photoresistor, 34. Spring roller of the first shutter blind, 35. Battery test button, 36. Printed circuit, 37. Film rewind crank.

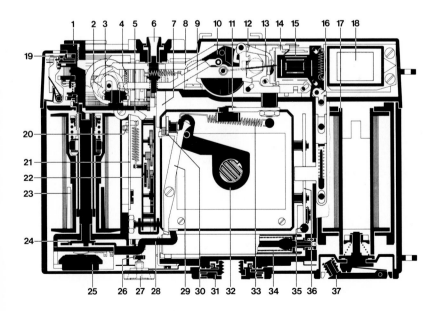

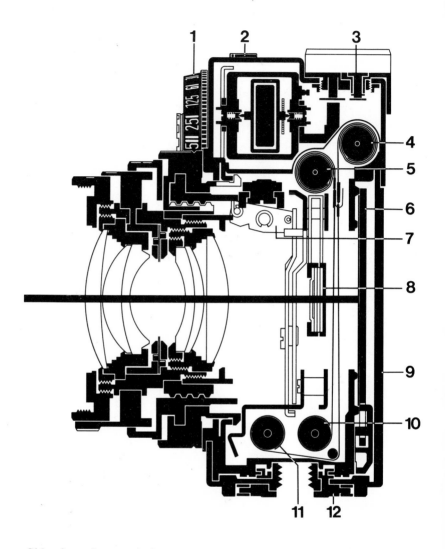

Side view of cross section

The focal plane shutter consists of two blinds which run from the rollers (4) and (5) vertically down to the rollers (10 and 11). Pressure on the release button (2) causes the photoresistor (8) to swing out via the lever (7) and releases the shutter.

The shutter speeds are set by means of the ring (1) after setting the film speed. The shutter is synchronized through the X-centre contact (3).

For loading film into the camera the catch (12) is turned to the left and the camera back and base (9) pulled off downwards. The film pressure plate (6) must be swung down for loading.

Sectional view of viewfinder and rangefinder

The range-viewfinder combines the functions of split image and coincidence rangefinder. The rangefinder observation field lies roughly in the centre of the viewfinder field. In use, the sliding lens element (6) in its frame (12) is moved horizontally sideways by the rangefinder lever. The control beam (5) passes first through the lens (7) and is deflected and inverted by the prism (14). After passing the sliding lens (6) it meets the field lens (9) and passes to the eye through the eyepiece lens (10) where its image is superimposed upon that produced by the finder beam (1) which has passed through the front lens (2). The semi-transparent mirror (8) superimposes the viewfinder and rangefinder images. The frame reflector (11) simultaneously reflects the luminous frames through the semi-transparent mirror (8) into the eye. In accordance with the focal length of the camera lens in use, the frame plate (4) is covered by the masking plate (3).

Parallax is automatically compensated in focusing. To this end the luminous frame plate (4) is displaced on the masking plate (3) and the rangefinder field mask (13).

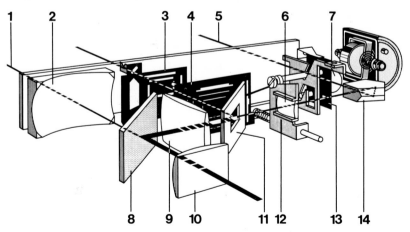

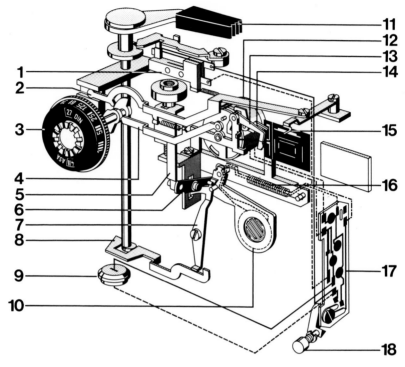

The exposure meter

Directly in front of the vertically running shutter is the CdS photoresistor (10) which measures selectively the light falling on the centre of the picture area through the camera lens. The photoresistor is electrically connected through the printed control circuit (17) with the galvanometer (12). The measurement is made by rotating the shutter speed ring (3) so that the pointer coincides with the central notch in the viewfinder field. This is effected by means of a cam which moves the lever (4) and rotates the galvanometer. Simultaneously the linkage (2) is actuated by a second cam which adjusts the position of the shutter speed pointer (15) to show on the viewfinder scale the shutter speed which has been set. By swinging out the rapid wind lever (11) the switch (1) closes the circuit of the meter system, which is fed by the button cell (9).

The battery test is carried out by setting the shutter speed dial to 1/60 sec, which brings a black marker into the shutter speed read-out strip. Now, pressure on the battery test button (18) brings the meter needle into the correct exposure notch if the battery is functioning correctly. A red warning signal on the lever (13) likewise appears in this central notch if the camera is not operative because light conditions are below the meter range.

Pressure on the release frees the photoresistor through the slide bar (5) and lever (6). The photoresistor springs sideways out of the light path, operated by the tension spring (16), and shortly before reaching its final position releases the shutter via the aforementioned lever and slide bar. When the rapid wind lever is operated, the levers (7) and (8) swing back the photoresistor to its operative position.

How the viewfinder works

The viewfinder consists of a negative front lens (13) and an eyepiece lens (8). A luminous frame mask system (12) behind the illuminating window of the camera is reflected in the frame mirror (5), and passes, through a convergent lens (6) and semi-transparent mirror (10) into the viewfinder optical system.

The luminous frame mask is controlled by several different elements. In inserting the lens, the lens mount operates the slide bar (22) to expose or cover the corresponding luminous frame.

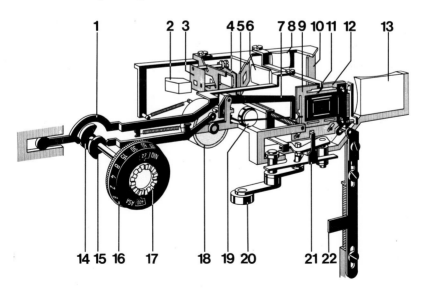

For parallax compensation, movement of the rangefinder roller (20), through the lever (21), causes the entire luminous frame system to move diagonally. The luminous frame plate has also a shutter speed scale for which the pointer (11) is connected, via the lever (1) and cam (14) to the shutter speed setting ring (16). A second cam (15), controlled by the film speed setting (17) on the shutter speed ring, switches on a red warning signal through the lever (7) in the finder when the exposure setting falls below the measuring range or if there is a failure in current supply. The galvanometer pointer is visible in the finder beside the format mask (9).

The measuring light beam of the rangefinder enters through the rangefinder window, passes through the lens (19) to the image erecting prism (2), where it is deflected and passes through the rangefinder mask (3). This moves diagonally and continuously with the format mask (parallax compensation) and is driven, through a lever, by the rangefinder roller (20), as also the rangefinder lens (4). This lens moves horizontally and links the measuring beam with the distance setting of the camera lens. The rangefinder beam then passes through the aperture of the mirror (5), and the convergent lens (6), and is deflected by the semi-transparent mirror (10) to the eyepiece (8) and so enters the eye.

THE LEICA CL SYSTEM

The Leica CL differs in two respects from many other compact cameras. First in its selective light measurement, and second in its use of the bayonet lens mount which permits interchange of lenses and brings the "CL" into the "system" class.

The advantages of the 24 x 36 mm can be fully exploited only if the best possible use can be made of the picture area. If less than 50% of that area is effectively utilized, the result is a noticeable loss of quality in the enlargement. Thus the facility for filling the format completely by the use of the most appropriate focal lengths for any viewpoint is of inestimable value.

Exhaustive market research has shown that with cameras having the interchangeable facility the vast proportion of exposures made fall within two groups.

The reason for this is very simple, we look at the world in similar fashion. First we take a general look, corresponding to the use of a wide angle lens in the camera (35 — 40 mm), and then we occupy ourselves with a close study of interesting detail. This much smaller area of the subject is most conveniently embraced with a telephoto lens (90 mm).

The two lenses which have been specially developed for the Leica CL: the Summicron-C f/2, 40 mm, and the Elmar-C f/4, 90 mm.

Both photographs by Gunter Osterloh

A wide angle is a universal lens for travel and many other purposes. Wide field of view — great depth of field — and with a high light transmission; small and light — quick to operate. In many cases it can be effectively employed without even a glance in the viewfinder.

Wide angle lenses emphasize the foreground. Lines which lead into the picture converge very rapidly, thereby enhancing the impression of space. On the other hand details in the background are rendered very small.

With so wide an angle of view, in some cases a great deal of detail is embraced, which by its very complexity and small scale reproduction is not really satisfactory.

It is for this reason that a second lens, with a considerably smaller angle of view, is so valuable. From the same viewpoint we embrace only a fraction of the wide angle scene, but this is reproduced on a correspondingly larger

46

There are many occasions similar to the above in which it is not possible freely to choose one's viewpoint. Certainly the picture taken with the 40 mm lens gives quite a good general view, but only the 90 mm lens can convey the tension inherent in the incident.

scale. The very small depth of field results in better spatial differentiation. Since, moreover, fewer lines and shapes are involved, these can be better aranged in the picture space.

More convincing than any words, however, are the pictures reproduced on these two pages which illustrate the practical significance of this difference in focal length. The viewpoint was not 100% the same for the two photographs, but the difference had practically no effect on the result.

If a camera is to be equipped with two lenses of different focal lengths, then the difference between them should be so great as to present totally different pictorial potentialities. This is clearly the case with the 40 mm and 90 mm lenses. While in some situations a wide angle lens is indispensable, in others a handy telephoto can be just as valuable. 90 mm is, of course, not in the extreme long focus class.

47

Summicron-C f/2, 40 mm

Elmar-C f/4, 90 mm

Summicron-C f/2, 40 mm

Technical data:

Construction: Gauss type, 6 elements, 4 components.

Field of view: 57⁰ diagonal.

Apertures: f/2 — f/16, click stops, including half values.

Filter series: 5.5 (see page 52).

Combined feet-metre focusing scale.

Focusing range: infinity to 0.8 metre.

Smallest object field: 43 x 65 cm.

Length: 23.5 mm (from bayonet support).

Maximum diameter: 51 mm.

Weight, including lens hood: 130 gm.

Lens hood: Order No. for replacement: 12518.

Lens cap: fits into the collapsible lens hood (O/No. 14191).

Screw thread of lens front mount: M 39 x 0.75 (this does not correspond to the filter screw thread Leitz E 39).

These technical data clearly show that the quality of this lens in light transmission and performance, dimensions and weight, is of a very high rating. It is a wide angle lens, its angular field of view being 57⁰. The average field of such lenses lies between 40⁰ and 50⁰. It is, however, by no means an extreme wide angle. Its wide initial aperture of f/2 will be found useful on many occasions. Used in conjunction with a high speed film (400 ASA) it is almost always possible to make hand-held exposures in ordinary room lighting. At full aperture, of course, special care must be taken to focus accurately, but it dispenses with the need for flash.

Elmar-C f/4, 90 mm

Technical data:
Construction: modified triplet, 4 elements.
Field of view: 27^0 diagonal.
Apertures: f/4 to f/22 click stops including half values.
Filter series: 5-5 (see page 52).
Combined feet-metre focusing scale.
Focusing range: infinity to 1 metre.
Smallest object field: 22 x 33 cm.
Length: 61 mm (from bayonet support).
Maximum diameter: 51 mm.
Weight, including lens hood: 265 gm.
Lens hood: Order No. for replacement; 12517.
Lens cap: fits into the collapsible lens hood. (O/No. 14191)
Screw thread of lens mount: M 39 x 0.75 (this does not correspond to the filter screw thread Leitz E 39).

A focal length of 90 mm is an ideal compromise for the 24 x 36 mm format; it calls for concentration on framing, the depth of field is smaller, so that details do not crowd up together. At the closest working distance (1 metre) it gives a scale of reproduction of 1:9 (approximately DIN A4 paper size) which suffices in many cases for a detailed record. Used at distances from 1.25 to 1.5 metres it gives satisfactory perspective in portraits.

It is useful in practice to be able to visualize the angle of view of a lens. It is comparatively easy to acquire this facility if we familiarize ourselves with the rules of image formation. There is a definite relation between focal length and working distance. To avoid undue complication in calculation the formula can be somewhat simplified: the resulting error is small if in the case of a 40 mm lens we rule out working distances of less than 2 metres. The formula then reads $\frac{f}{u}$ = R where f = focal length, u = distance, R = scale of reproduction.

For example: $\frac{40 \text{ mm}}{4000 \text{ mm}} = \frac{1}{100}$ i.e. with a 40mm lens at 4 metres subject distance the scale of reproduction will be 1/100 the original size. Suppose we are photographing a brick wall, we shall thus cover an area of 2.4 x 3.6 metres. The area shown in the viewfinder is very slightly less than will be recorded on the film.

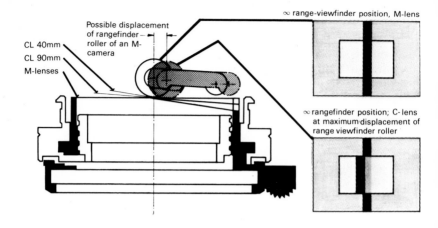

∞ range-viewfinder position, M-lens

Possible displacement
of rangefinder —
roller of an M-
camera

CL 40mm
CL 90mm
M-lenses

∞ rangefinder position; C-lens
at maximum displacement of
range viewfinder roller

CL lenses on Leica-M cameras

Screw-mount Leica lenses and bayonet mount lenses for the Leica-M
cameras have a differential helical motion, i.e. the contact surface for the
range-finder roller is displaced parallel in focusing. In order to achieve a
compact, light construction with the Summicron-C f/2, 40 mm and Elmar-
C f/4, 90 mm lenses for the CL this system was dispensed with. Both the
CL lenses have high curvatures. Consequently, although they can certainly
be used on the M-cameras it is possible that the rangefinder will in some
cases show certain small inaccuracies. Before using the CL lenses on M
bodies, therefore, you should check whether the rangefinder control is
accurate. The thing to check is whether at infinity setting the two images
are perfectly in register.

Coating

For years past, all Leitz lenses have been "coated". This means that they
have been given a brownish-violet shimmering coating which enhances
light transmission and image brilliance.

These anti-reflection coatings are produced by evaporation in a high
vacuum. Whereas the reflection value of an uncoated surface is from 4 to
7% it is reduced by coating to 1% or less. The coatings on the exterior
surfaces of the lens are resistant to damage by cleaning.

The care of lenses

From time to time check whether the lens surfaces are immaculately clean, since only this will ensure brilliant photographs. If a surface exhibits any traces of dirt, first remove any loose dust with a soft brush and then clean it carefully with a cotton cloth (handkerchief) which has been repeatedly washed, or with special lens-cleaning paper. Traces of grease can be removed with a few drops of pure alcohol on a handkerchief.

The special cleaning cloths such as are used for cleaning spectacles are not recommended for this purpose, because they are impregnated with chemical substances which could attack the glasses of camera lenses.

When a camera is used in the presence of seawater, the front lens should be protected with a colourless UV (ultra-violet) filter against splashes of seawater or sand. The filter is easier to clean than a camera lens.

When taking night photographs in which street lights appear, no filter should be used, since the addition of the plane-parallel glass filter can result in undesirable reflections. The intensity of such light sources is so high that their reflected images become visible in the shadows.

Young crocodile. At a distance of 80 cm at f/2.8 it is important to locate the plane of sharp focus in the right place, for depth of field is very small.

Series filters

Series filters differ from the earlier screw-in filters in having a flat mount with no screw thread. They are simply placed on the lens and are held in place by the lens hood. The diameters of the series filters are standardized.

No Leitz filters are supplied for Compact lenses. The usual yellow, green, orange, and red filters are intended only for black-and-white films, and are rapidly becoming out-of-date. The vast majority of photographs taken today are on colour film, and suitable filters for use with these are always available from the film manufacturers or from special suppliers.

To attach a filter of Series 5.5 (diameter 36 mm) the lens hood is unscrewed and the filter so placed on the lens that it will be held in place by the lens hood when this is screwed on again (see illustration). When screwing on and unscrewing, the lens should be held somewhat downwards, so that the filter cannot fall.

The use of the filters is explained in the following chapter. The screw thread on the front lens mount of the CL lens is M39 x 0.75. It does not correspond to the thread of the Leica filters E 39.

Filters for black-and-white films

The original photographic emulsions were sensitive only to light from the ultra-violet as far as the blue, and there are still today some "unsensitized" emulsions designed for special use. They reproduce blue almost as white, but red appears black. The reverse, in fact, to one's normal visual impression. Such emulsions do not require the use of filters.

By adding certain dyes in emulsion manufacture the emulsions become sensitive to colour. Films which are thus sensitized to all colours except red are termed "orthochromatic"; "panchromatic" films are sensitive also to red.

Even in black-and-white photography however one speaks of colour sensitivity, although they do not reproduce the actual colours, but only a lighter or darker grey rendering of them. In this way, two colours such as green and red or yellow and blue which in nature exhibit striking colour contrasts can in some circumstances be rendered, in a photograph, as practically identical tones of grey. A more realistic rendering can be achieved by the use of suitable filters. In choosing such a filter one must consider the effect, not on the visual image, but on the photographic material. Any colour filter has the property of transmitting most efficiently light of its own colour, and suppressing, more or less, according to its density, the transmission of light of the "opposite" colour — its "complementary". Thus, for example, a yellow filter will cause a film to render yellow in lighter shade of grey; blue, on the contrary, it will render darker. (A few comparative test exposures will quickly establish this).

YELLOW FILTERS

A yellow filter is indispensable for snow scenes, otherwise despite the sunshine shadows on the snow surface would come out much too flat. In landscape photography, too, it is useful, in order to show up better white clouds against a blue sky. The exposure increase factor, which as a rule is given as 2, can be used with a normal reading, but in snowscapes and bright landscapes a correct reading is possible only by making a selective measurement.

ORANGE FILTER

This is a favourite filter, emphasizing somewhat, as it does, differential tone values in black-and-white photography. The contrast of blue sky and white clouds is strikingly increased, as also the shadows in snow scenes.

Landscape at Fiss (Tirol); Left: without; Right: with polarizing filter.

Filters for black-and-white and colour films

UVa FILTER (COLOURLESS)

UVa signifies "ultra-violet absorbing", and this filter eliminates the invisible ultra-violet radiation. Its main use is in colour photography. It can be left permanently on the lens, since it has no unwanted effects, and at the same time provides very effective protection of the front lens against dirt, sand, or sea spray.

One exception should be noted: in night photography, when very intense light sources appear in the picture, the polished surfaces of the filter can cause reflections. Even though such reflected images represent only a fraction of the total light emission, their presence in the shadow areas can often be very disturbing.

POLARIZING FILTER

This is an interesting filter. It was used originally for eliminating reflections from polished surfaces. This property however exists only for particular reflection angles, and also only for non-metallic surfaces, and in the past, therefore, the use of the filter was not very extensive.

However another source of polarized light is found, at certain angles, in the sky, and as a result the polarizing filter has found wide use in landscape photography. Clouds can be made to stand out better from blue sky, and the distance be rendered clearer and with greater contrast. Their effect in colour photography somewhat resembles the use of yellow or orange filters in black-and-white.

Only the neutral grey type of filter can be used for colour photography. The effect of the filter can be controlled visually: the filter is rotated slowly in front of the eye until the best effect is seen. It is then transferred, in the same orientation, to the camera lens. The exposure increase required is automatically taken into account by the Leica CL.

Filters for colour films

In colour photography filters are for the most part used in a different way from black-and-white. The only ones in common are the UVa and the polarizing filter. Depending upon the purpose involved, there are two types of filter used in colour photography.

CONVERSION FILTERS

Reversal films are manufactured for use with daylight ($5600^{\circ}K$), or with tungsten lighting ($3200^{\circ}K$). By the use of conversion filters each type of colour film can be used with the other kind of lighting. It has been found very satisfactory in practice to use artificial light film throughout, with, for daylight use, as conversion filter, either the KR-12, a solid glass filter, or the Kodak film filter No. 85B. The results are good: with the Kodak filter there is no loss of speed, because the artificial light film is 2 DIN/1.2 ASA faster than the corresponding daylight film. With the KR-12 filter there is a loss of speed of half a stop. In order to obtain correct exposure measurement through the lens, the film speed setting knob should be set to 1—2 DIN/1—1.2 ASA lower than the film speed specified by the manufacturer.

The other alternative, using a daylight film for artificial light, requires the solid glass filter KB-12 or the Kodak film filter 80B. The exposure increase factor for the filter has then in both cases to be taken into account. This procedure will in practice only be adopted in exceptional cases, since it involves an effective film speed loss of 6 DIN/3ASA, or two stops.

Compatibility with the Leica system

The Leica CL has the same bayonet lens interchange facility as the Leica-M models. This enables a whole range of Leica-M lenses and some of its accessories to be used with the CL (see illustration above). Screw mounted lenses and accessories also can be adapted by means of bayonet adapters (No. 14097 for 50 mm, 14908 for 28 and 90 mm, 14099 for 35 mm focus).

There are some limitations, which are due to the smaller size of the Leica CL camera body, the shorter rangefinder base, and the fact that the photocell swings in front of the focal plane shutter. Below, we give details of these limitations, and also of the cases in which adaptation is not possible. In this, the perfect functioning of the exposure meter has been specially borne in mind.

When does the lens hood interfere in close-up work?

Because the Leica CL is considerably smaller, the rangefinder window is closer to the camera lens axis than in the Leica-M models. With certain lenses this results in a partial obstruction of the rangefinder window if the lens hood is used in close-up photography. A shadow is caused if anything interferes with the direct view from the viewfinder; the format frames then appear against a dark background, the rangefinder remaining open in the centre.

If the centre of the field is directed at a bright surface, any shadows which may be present will disappear if the lens hood is removed.

When using the wide aperture 50 mm lenses Summilux f/1.4 and Noctilux f/1.0 or f/1.2 at full aperture an effective rangefinder base of 19 mm is rather short. The lens should therefore be stopped down at least to f/2.

Lenses with a minimum focusing distance below 0.8 metre

Since the rangefinder of the Leica CL has a minimum focusing range of 0.8 metre, distances shorter than this cannot be focused with the rangefinder. Naturally the lenses can still be used by measuring the working distance with a tape measure. All distances are related to the film plane (distance to camera back minus 5 mm).

Deep seated Leica lenses

The fact that the photocell swings into the light path limits the free space in the camera interior. Deep seated Leica lenses which penetrate into this space must be prevented from entering too far by attaching an adhesive protective band. In the case of the Leica CL, lenses must not penetrate more than 16 mm — measured from the lens supporting surface. In the case of the Leica M5 it is limited to only 13 mm. The width of the protective band needed is thus dependent upon whether the lens is to be used only with the Leica CL or also with a Leica M5.

The Dymo band limits lens penetration into camera body

The adhesive strip used should be 6.3 mm wide or — if it is to be used also with the Leica M5 — 9.5 mm, and is attached to the lens mount as shown in the illustration. The deep seated Summicron f/2, 50 mm lenses mostly do not need this band. On the other hand the Hektor f/2.5, 50 mm needs a 9.5 mm band for the Leica CL and a 12.7 mm band for the Leica M5. This strip material is available from stationers. It is used in a small embossing machine for making name plates. It is self adhesive and should be so cut as to wrap completely round the lens mount leaving a gap of only about 1 mm. To be sure as to length, it is convenient first to make a paper gauge to the correct length.

It is of course possible to use only the 6.3 mm wide strip, provided this is attached correspondingly lower on the lens mount. This calls for a certain amount of dexterity, since there is the no upper edge to act as a guide.

The viewfinder of the Leica CL is provided with luminous frames for 40, 50, and 90 mm focal length. With other lenses a brilliant finder is necessary (28 mm Order No. 12007; 35 mm No. 12010).

Lenses of which the rear mount projects too deeply into the camera body are not suitable for use with the Leica CL (Super-Angulon 21 mm, Hologon f/8, 15 mm, Elmarit f/2.8, 28 mm with serial numbers below 2 314 921); also lenses with finder attachment, such as the 35 mm wide angle lenses for the Leica M3 and the Elmarit f/2.8, 135 mm. The Summicron f/2, 90 mm and the other 135 mm lenses can certainly be used, but only with reservations.

Some accessories, too, cannot be used, where the attachment dimensions fit only the Leica, as for instance optical close-up focusing attachments, slide copiers, the Reprovit I to IIa, and Visoflex III.

Close-up attachments*

Very suitable for still close-up work are the close-up focusing accessories. These comprise the DIN-A4, DIN-A5, and DIN-A6 equipment (16526) of the M system, and the close-up accessory for 1:1 to 1:3 (16511). Also, in the screw mount system the copying gauge accessories BOOWU, BEHOO, and BELUN (-HESUM)

----

*Further details on page 123 in the chapter on close-up photography.

The Visoflex reflex housing can be used without reservation provided a tripod is employed. Note that the mirror must be swung up for exposure determination. If in the Leica CL viewfinder the measuring field is covered, we use the small circle in the centre of the ground glass of the Visoflex I for orientation.

The Visoflex II can certainly be used, but its manipulation is complicated and therefore not altogether recommended.

Photomicrography

In normal transmitted light, bright field microscopy exposure determination can be carried out with the built-in exposure meter of the Leica CL. Selective measurement of a limited area gives greater accuracy, which is very useful especially in photomicrography. In all photomicrographic investigations at low light intensities (dark field, fluorescence, polarization) the special Microsix exposure meter is, as always, to be recommended.

Adaptation to the microscope is effected with the Leica M adapter (Order No. 543195).

Sensitive materials

There is a very wide range of films which can be used with the Leica CL, taking as it does the standard 24 x 36 mm cassette. This may well be confusing to the beginner: the experienced photographer welcomes this wide choice as a great advantage.

To choose wisely it is necessary to understand clearly the individual characteristics of the various films. Fundamentally, of course, they fall into two main categories: black-and-white and colour. In the course of the last ten years far more colour photographs have been taken than black-and-white. There are two reasons for this: machine produced colour prints have been greatly improved in quality, and at the same time have become cheaper because of the enormous increase in quantity. The reverse has happened to black-and-white: reduced demand, often mediocre quality, with increasing price. Colour today is the norm, and if here we give priority to the characteristics of colour film we are merely following general practice. It is true that black-and-white films are simpler in construction, but for the amateur they are more difficult to use successfully, because the diversity of natural colours has to be expressed in shades of grey. On the other hand anyone who intends to do his own processing should begin with black-and-white and only after some experience with it venture on the rather more complex business of colour processing.

Only standard commercial, not Leica metal cassettes

Only standard commercial cassettes can be used in the Leica CL, not the Leica metal cassettes. They are available in either 20 or 36 exposures. In them, the film is wound on the central core with the emulsion side inwards. The outer casing may be of sheet metal or plastic. The slot through which the film is withdrawn is lined with velvet or felt; it is not absolutely light tight and cassettes, either new or exposed, should therefore not be left lying around exposed to the light. After the last exposure has been made the film has to be rewound into the cassette in order that it may be safely removed from the camera in full light. It is not advisable to reload cassettes from bulk film. This procedure calls for a great deal of skill and absolute cleanliness, and the saving in cost is only worth while if time is of no account.

No other format offers so great a choice of films with a wealth of different characteristics. Throughout the whole world miniature cassettes form the bulk of films on sale.

Kittens love to play; it is easy, if we find anyone playing with them, to secure a series of photographs. 400 ASA film, 1/60 sec.

The advantages of the 24 x 36 mm format

The Leica cassette takes up to 36 exposures. Its weight is insignificant, and the cost so low that one need never hesitate at taking a picture. We can feel free to photograph the same subject from a variety of viewpoints, or to experiment with a dozen shots in recording movement, in order to secure the best aspect.

Only the small format permits full advantage to be taken of the high light transmission of wide aperture lenses. The broad perforated border ensures that the film lies flat. As the result of technical development and the consequent improvement in film quality, the minature format has now become a "medium" format. At the same time the reduction in over-all size of the Leica CL has achieved for it a handiness which makes it ideal for many branches of photography.

How long will films keep?

Photographic emulsions have only limited keeping properties. Every film sold bears on the outside carton the emulsion number and its expiry date, and no responsibility will be accepted by the manufacturer for a film kept beyond this date. In case of complaint the carton should be returned with the film.

The conditions of storage are important to a film's keeping quality. The best conditions are cool and dry; moisture is harmful, above all at high temperatures. Continual change of conditions also reduces length of life. If the film is kept very cool, the life will extend beyond the expiry date. A suitable place to keep films is in the vegetable compartment of a refrigerator, stored in plastic containers. The temperature there will be about 8 — 10^{0}C, and at this temperature the film can be used right away. Stored in a deep freeze, the keeping quality is still better, but the film must be taken out 6 hours before use, to enable it to return to normal temperature. At deep freeze temperatures it is hard and brittle.

Time-expired black-and-white films are still usable, provided their speed is rated somewhat lower (about 3 DIN/1.5ASA). In the case of colour films which have been kept too long or at too high a temperature, it is less easy to forecast what effect this will have, because the colour balance of the three layers will have been disturbed. So far as colour negative films are concerned, any error thus introduced can always be corrected in printing; colour reversal films on the other hand may show a colour cast.

A particularly disturbing situation arises when a colour film has been kept too long — for some months — in the camera before sending it for processing: the "latent" image, as it is termed, where the film has been exposed but not processed, becomes weaker on storage, so that it behaves as though underexposed. This effect, likewise, is not identical in the three layers, so that a colour shift becomes apparent. Colour films, therefore, should always be completely exposed within a matter of weeks and immediately sent for processing.

How can transport hazards to our precious colour reversal films be minimized? At many central postal collection stations, thousands of films are received each year whose senders cannot be identified. Take the precaution, therefore, of photographing on the first frame an A4 (210 x 297 mm/8¼ x 11¾in.) sheet of paper carrying your name and address in bold print. The original can be folded up and carried in the camera case and when required spread on the ground out of doors and photographed.

62

COLOUR PHOTOGRAPHY

Colour photographs can be taken with any Leica CL. The fact that colour is actually reproduced is merely a matter of the sensitive material used. In many cases it is simpler to produce a colour photograph than a black-and-white one. Admittedly some extra care needs to be taken in regard to lighting and correct exposure, but with the selective exposure system of the Leica CL, exposure, at least, presents no problem.

The manufacture of colour film is a phenomenal technical achievement, but even so small deviations in the final result are unavoidable, and in particular this can be the result of storage or variations in processing. To reduce such deviations to a minimum, therefore, certain factors which are known adversely to affect quality should be studiously avoided. Thus it is important to keep films cool, in a refrigerator, not to leave them for months in the camera, and to send them for processing as soon as possible after exposure.

For successful colour photography it is not necessary to understand all the details of its physical and chemical basis. It is sufficient to know the principle on which the colours are analysed and subsequently re-established, and to appreciate that colour film responds more relentlessly than the eye to variations in the spectral composition of the lighting. Further details will be found in the chapter on "Colour temperature".

White light is a mixture of coloured light, as can be clearly seen when we analyse the light into its component colours by passing it through a prism. Modern colour films have at least three differently sensitized emulsion layers superimposed, thus enabling the spectral composition to be analysed into its three basic components — blue, green, and red. Reproduction is effected by subtractive colour mixing.

Additive and subtractive colour mixing

In *additive* colour mixing, two or more coloured lights are combined to form one colour — e.g. green and red light superimposed produce yellow. Any colour can be reproduced by mixing the primary colours blue, green, and red in suitable proportions, but this can only be done with coloured *light*.

In *subtractive* colour mixing, light passes successively through one or more light filters, each of which absorbs a part of the light, while allowing the rest to pass through. To enable all colours to be reproduced, the filter colours yellow, magenta, and cyan are so adjusted that each filter absorbs one third of the light while transmitting the remaining two thirds.

Yellow absorbs blue, transmitting green and red.

Magenta absorbs green, transmitting blue and red.

Cyan (blue-green) absorbs red, transmitting blue and green.

If the light passes successively through two of the filters, it will transmit only a third of the spectrum.

Yellow and magenta absorb blue and green, transmitting red.

Yellow and cyan absorb blue and red, transmitting green.

Magenta and cyan absorb green and red, transmitting blue.

If all three filters are superposed, all three spectral regions will be absorbed, and the result will be black.

How is the colour produced in colour film?

Colour films have three superimposed emulsion layers: the topmost layer is blue sensitive, the middle one green sensitive, and the bottom one red sensitive. To ensure that no blue light shall reach the green and red sensitive layers, a deep yellow filter layer is interposed beneath the top layer.

In the course of processing, dyes are formed in the three layers: in accordance with the subtractive principle, a yellow dye in the top, blue sensitive layer, and magenta and cyan respectively in the middle and bottom layers. Each layer of the film is responsible for only one third of the spectrum. Colour mixing occurs only when two layers participate. In reproducing grey and black, all three layers take part.

Reversal and negative films are basically similar, but there are important differences in their use and processing.

Colour reversal film

In the colour reversal process, the image is converted, by a multi-stage processing procedure, direct into a positive transparency which can be projected on a screen. However it gives only the one single copy. For colour rendering, resolving power, and richness of tone it is unexcelled.

Paper prints can however be made from colour transparencies, but good results can be expected only if the original transparency is not too contrasty. In many cases a better quality print can be obtained if an "internegative" is first made, and from this colour prints. The cost of

Michael was photographed eating cherries indoors by ordinary daylight. His eyes are wide open. Elmar-C f/4, 1/30 sec.

64

good internegatives however is so high as to be worth while only in exceptional circumstances.

A distinction has to be made between reversal films whose processing cost is included in the purchase price of the film, and those which can be processed by the user (a course not recommended for the inexperienced) and to the purchase price of which has accordingly to be added the cost of user-processing.

There is also another alternative. When sending colour reversal films for processing, the processing laboratory will send them back, as desired, either in the original strip, or as ready-to-use slides in plastic or card frames. Glassless framing has become ever more popular, since it is well known that the durability of a colour transparency without glass is better than when it is framed between glass cover plates.

When using colour reversal film the exposure should be determined primarily by the lightest parts of the image in which detail is required. Transparencies which are underexposed are too dense, overexposed too light in tone. In the latter case the highlights are empty, or "burnt out".

The exposure latitude of reversal film is very small. It is therefore a great help that with the selective exposure measurement of the Leica CL it is possible to determine exposure very accurately. It is however necessary to be careful in our selection of the area which is suitable for measurement.

However it does happen now and again that an entire film comes out too light or too dark. This may be due to the very small tolerances both in manufacture and in processing, and on top of these may come the effects of storage. If all these factors fall in one direction, it is no fault of the camera if small deviations occur. Should you need rather lighter slides for large scale projection, the film speed setting on the camera should be made 1 — 2 DIN/1 — 1.2 ASA lower.

Daylight and artificial light colour film

There are two general types of reversal material: daylight film, balanced for a colour temperature (page 67) of 5600^0K, and artificial light film, balanced on the average for 3200^0K. Different films are needed because the colour rendering of the daylight film, if used for artificial light, deviates so widely from the normal visual colour impression that the transparencies are useless.

Tungsten lighting has a much smaller blue content than daylight. Artificial light film is consequently balanced to a higher blue sensitivity than daylight film. It can be used in daylight, provided it is adapted to the higher colour temperature of daylight by the use of a salmon coloured conversion filter. The use of the filter results in the loss of 2—3 DIN/1.2 — 1.5 ASA in effective emulsion speed, but the intrinsic higher sensitivity of the artificial light film almost completely compensates for this. On the other hand it is not advisable to use daylight film for artificial light: the deep blue filter which this calls for reduces the effective speed of the daylight film by about 6 DIN/3 ASA (see chapter on "Filters", page 53).

Colour negative film

In the three different colour sensitized emulsion layers of colour negative film there are produced, in processing, negative images in the subtractive primary colours yellow, magenta, and cyan. The final paper colour print or positive colour transparency is produced by a printing process similar to that of the film.

To improve colour rendering, intermediate layers, termed "masks", are included in the materials. There is no such thing as an ideal dye. The function of the masking layers is to correct the defective absorptions by means of a supplementary image. The absorption characteristics of the dyes used differ in the various makes of film. The masks conceal part of the colour content, but only so far as the eye is concerned. For the printing material, colour separation is fully preserved.

Colour negative material is always sold exclusive of the cost of processing. Mostly it is universal, and may be used either in daylight or by artificial light. Colour balance is corrected in printing.

Colour temperature

"Colour temperature" comes from physics terminology. It is a measure of the spectral composition of light, and is expressed in degrees Kelvin (^{0}K). It is in fact a Centigrade scale with its zero at the absolute zero of -273^{0}C. To determine the colour temperature of a light source we must know its spectral distribution.

Our most important light source is daylight. Under conditions of sunshine with scattered white clouds daylight has a colour temperature of about 5600^{0}K. Since the effective lighting in photography is a mixture of direct sunshine and scattered daylight, the colour temperature of this latter component plays an important role.

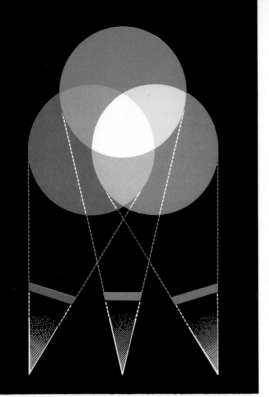

Additive colour mixing

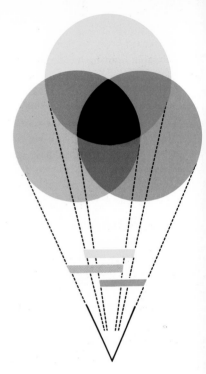

Subtractive colour mixing

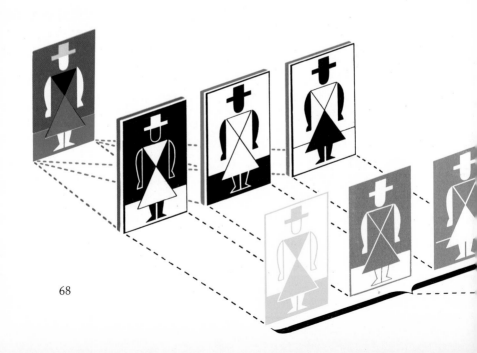

68

Arrangement of colour reversal film (Subtractive colour reproduction)

Top layer blue sensitive — later yellow
The yellow filter layer — becomes decolourized
Middle layer green sensitive — later magenta
Bottom layer red sensitive — later cyan
Anti-halation layer — is bleached out in processing

The shaded area is the film base

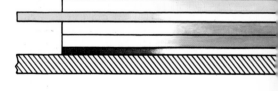

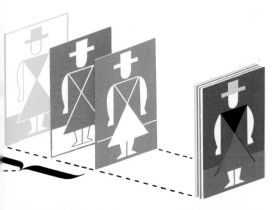

The separation images are produced in the blue, green, and red sensitive layers. Only the second development stage is carried out with dye coupled colour developers. The silver image simultaneously formed is bleached out, leaving only the colour image.

69

With deep blue sky at high altitudes (excluding direct sunlight) the colour temperature is about 27,000°K. The greater the blue content of light, the higher is the colour temperature. When the sun is low, on account of the long distance it has to travel through the atmosphere, the blue content of the light is greatly reduced, with the result that the light becomes yellowish or even reddish.

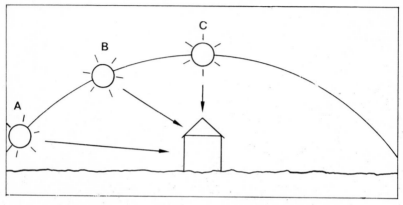

Height of sun above the horizon	A = 10°	B = 30°	C = 90°
Colour temperature in °Kelvin	3000	4500	5400

Our eyes very readily adapt themselves to changes in colour temperature. A sheet of white paper illuminated by tungsten lighting (2800°K) appears white, just as it does in sunlight (5600°K). Only when the two types of illumination appear together so that they can be compared does the difference become apparent. For example, if we look at a house, in a snow covered landscape, at dusk, the yellow colour of its lamp-lit windows is very apparent.

The table opposite gives some idea of the colour temperature of various light sources, the temperatures indicated being those which best coincide with the colour balance of daylight film (5600°K) and artificial light film (3200°K) respectively. (D) or (T)

Fluorescent lighting is not included in this table, since the spectrum of this type of lighting is not continuous, lacking some spectral colours altogether, and emphasizing other wavelengths. If, therefore, it forms the whole source of illumination, colour distortion is unavoidable. The distortion becomes less apparent if daylight or tungsten artificial lighting is also present to an amount of at least three times the fluorescent illumination.

DAYLIGHT in ⁰Kelvin (average values)

Skylight (blue)	10,000 — 30,000
Sunlight with white clouds	5600 (D)
Sunlight with blue sky	6000 — 9000
Sunlight at sunset	2500

ARTIFICIAL LIGHT

Candle light	1800 — 2000
Domestic tungsten lamps (60 — 100 watt)	2800
Nitraphot b	3100 (T)
Halogen lamps	3200 — 3400 (T)
Blue flash bulbs	6000 (D)
Electronic flash	6000 — 7000 (D)

(D) = daylight balanced films (T) = Artificial (tungsten) light films

Lighting contrast

In addition to colour temperature, lighting contrast plays an important part. Every photographic subject exhibits differences not only of colour but also of brightness, and this is influenced by the nature of the lighting. This light and shade effect is of dominant importance in black-and-white photography, but in colour photography should not be permitted to exceed a certain range. Colour rendering, for example, is adversely affected if the lighting contrast between the brightest and the darkest of the subject areas exceeds 4:1. This can be checked by holding a piece of white paper in the brightest area and taking a reading on the exposure meter, and repeating this on the darkest area. The difference in the two readings will give an idea of the contrast.

This lighting contrast has of course nothing to do with the over-all intrinsic brightness of the subject. A brightly illuminated snowscape may exhibit only a very low lighting contrast. On the other hand it is of great importance whether the photograph is taken by general lighting (with the sun behind the camera), with side lighting, or against the light. This last condition greatly increases lighting contrast, with the result that this may very easily overstep the capacity of the colour film. Such a thing will however not occur if, even in these contre-jour conditions, the shadows are well light, as is the case with snow scenes or beach photographs.

The following factors are, therefore, important for good colour rendering: 1. Colour temperature, 2. Lighting contrast, 3. Exposure.

This puffin was photographed by Julius Behnke, during a trip to Iceland, with the Elmar-C 90 mm.

The characteristics of black-and-white films

GENERAL SENSITIVITY

Since correct exposure depends upon film sensitivity, we must know the characteristics of the film we are using. In Germany, film speed is expressed in degrees DIN. The DIN scale is so devised that the speed doubles for every 3 degrees increase in the DIN number. Conversely 3 degrees lower DIN number halves the speed. The tolerance in speed allowed by manufacturers is 1 DIN (1ASA). The measurement is in accordance with the German standard DIN 4512 Sheet 1, and is based on mean values for contrast and subject range.

The internationally recognized speed system is the American ASA. On this system the speed number is proportional to the speed, i.e. doubling the speed doubles the ASA number. With the Leica CL the film speed can be set direct to either system. For conversion, a convenient aide memoire is the equivalence relation: 21 DIN = 100 ASA.

The effective film speed can be increased by prolonging development, but at the same time this increases contrast. Under normal exposure conditions it is not advisable to resort to this facility. Only when light conditions are so bad as to enforce underexposure to the limit should one have recourse to it.

SENSITIZING, COLOUR SENSITIVITY

The expression colour sensitivity, paradoxically, is used only in connection with black-and-white film. Unsensitized photographic emulsions are sensitive only up to 500 nm (blue light). By the addition of selected dyes in emulsion manufacture it can be made sensitive to other spectral ranges. Orthochromatic films are sensitive also to green and yellow. In panchromatic films sensitivity extends to all colours, including red. Infra-red films are sensitized even for wavelengths to which the eyes are not sensitive.

It is not easy for the beginner to visualize the grey brightness equivalent of colours. Thus in some circumstances highly contrasting colours such as red and green may appear almost identical when rendered in their equivalent greys in a photograph. Add to this, that these greys would not in any case agree with the visual impression because in daylight the film is over-sensitive to blue and violet. If for example we photograph a blue sky with white clouds, the result will correspond with the visual impression only if this over-sensitivity to blue is reduced by using on the camera lens a yellow or orange filter. Further information as to the influence of filters on colour rendering in black-and-white will be found on page 53 in the chapter on Filters.

For these reasons it is advisable to concentrate more on lighting contrast, light and shade, because these are in any case retained in the resultant grey rendering. How this can then be further improved in regard to picture composition by the characteristics of the film, its processing, and manipulation in printing, is dealt with in the following section on Gradation.

GRADATION

Gradation signifies the density distribution throughout the scale of tones. For most photography we need emulsions which will perfectly reproduce all degrees of brightness from the most brilliant white to the deepest black. Such films are said to have normal gradation. The gradation can of course be controlled by varying development time. If development is curtailed, the gradation can be flattened, i.e. the contrast reduced. If prolonged, the negative contrast is increased. A soft gradation film reduces the contrast between individual tone values and so can embrace a greater over-all subject contrast. A hard gradation film strengthens small steps in the scale of tones, and so imparts brilliance to inherently low contrast subjects. At the same time this makes it impossible for it to give a correct tone rendering of subjects of higher contrast.

For scientific recording of gradation, the logarithm of density is plotted as a curve — the "characteristic curve" of the emulsion. The same method is also employed to evaluate the characteristics of developers. The steeper this curve, the more contrasty is the film. For the amateur to whom the equipment for densitometric measurement is not available, the usual "gamma" values are of theoretical interest only. The serious photographer may find it more useful to photograph a grey scale under controlled conditions. By comparing the "standard" negative thus obtained with that from any subsequent film it can be quickly determined whether the film is "soft", "normal", or "hard".

If need be such a grey scale can be home made, but a more accurate judgement is provided by the standard Repro grey wedge (DIN 16543) as used in the graphic industry. The graphic technical departments of Agfa-Gevaert and Kodak supply such grey wedges, some of them in conjunction with a colour scale.

74

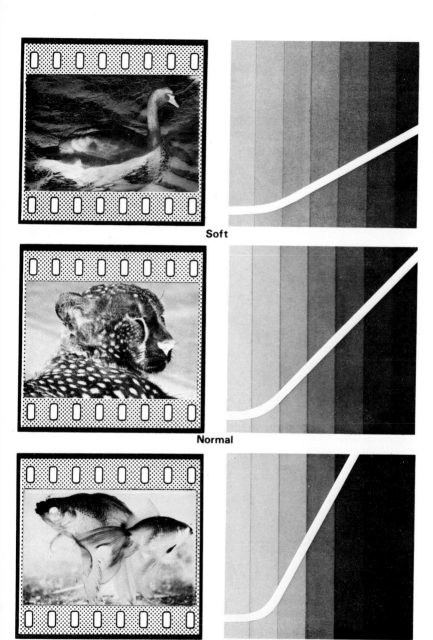

Soft

Normal

Hard

75

RESOLUTION AND GRAININESS

Under the microscope, that is to say viewed at a relatively high magnification, a developed black-and-white film exhibits an irregular grain structure. The original silver bromide crystals are reduced by the process of development to grains of metallic silver, which tend to coalesce — "clumping", as it is termed — and the larger the original crystals, and the more energetic the development, the greater is the clumping.

The thickness of the emulsion is an important factor, and there is a relation between the sensitivity of the silver bromide crystals and their size. In general, very high speed emulsions exhibit a coarser structure than those of lower sensitivity. Also the method of manufacture plays a part, and high speed film from manufacturer A may exhibit finer grain structure than even a somewhat less sensitive film from manufacturer B.

By resolving power is understood the capability of the film to reproduce extremely fine, closely adjacent detail as separate and distinguishable. In this, the nature of the graininess plays an important role. On one and the same film the graininess may be more, or less, apparent. The reason for this lies in the subject contrast. Areas of uniform tone exhibit grain structure more than areas without detail, while the graininess of ultra-speed films is more evident with full than with normal exposure. The maximum resolution and finest grain are produced by what are known as document films. These are of very low speed and very high contrast, but are, up to a point, adaptable by suitable development.

Excessive exposure reduces the resolution of a film, and also introduces light diffusion effects. This is clearly shown by the x40 comparison enlargements reproduced below.

The better the anti-halation protection of a film, the less edge detail is lost at relatively high contrasts, as is evident from this example, taken at the Westerland artificial wave swimming bath, with its enormous windows.

FREEDOM FROM HALATION, CONTOUR SHARPNESS

A photographic material is a turbid medium. If there are high contrasts in the subject, lateral light scatter can occur within it, as for instance at the edge of light sources. This scatter can never be completely avoided, but can be much reduced if the film is provided with an anti-halation layer.

A distinction must be made between light scatter and halation, which arises from reflection from the film base. The former is due to inter-reflection between the emulsion particles, and is least apparent in very thinly coated emulsions.

There are a number of ways of minimizing halation, such as the blue-grey colouration of the base, a protective dye in the emulsion itself, a dyed inter-mediate layer between the photographic emulsion and the base, and a coloured back coating. These may also be used in various combinations.

Correct exposure minimizes light scatter, overexposure greatly exaggerates it.

An objective criterion of the definition characteristics of a film is contour sharpness, and light scatter has a very great effect on this. Contour sharpness, is determined by means of a slit 15/1000 mm wide. The film is brought into contact with this slit, and, through it, exposed to light. The broadening of the developed image thus produced is measured, and this measurement constitutes the contour sharpness criterion.

Correct choice of film

It is not altogether easy, from among the wide range of black-and-white films available, to choose the best for your purpose. Subjects vary widely in character, and since a cassette comprises up to 36 frames, it is not possible to adapt the film to suit any exceptional circumstances.

For holiday purposes the best choice is a universal film of 20-24 DIN/80-200 ASA speed which is quite fast enough for landscapes, street scenes, and even well light interiors. It cannot claim extreme sensitivity or resolving power, but over all it does offer an optimum range of potentialities.

For years past it has been common practice to acquaint oneself with what the "professional", the Press photographer, uses. For almost every purpose he in fact uses a 27 DIN/400 ASA film. The results are astonishingly good, provided the format is well chosen for the subject and exposure and development are correctly adjusted. Press photographers however very rarely take landscape pictures, and in these such films display a certain graininess, most conspicuous in the uniform tonal areas of the sky. The degree of enlargement, too, obviously plays a part. Graininess is less disturbing in 9 x 13 cm album prints than in 30 x 40 cm display enlargements.

Fundamentally, there is only one way of getting to know more about a film, and that is to use it; expose text films, which serve three purposes: improving our facility with the handling of the camera, increasing our appreciation of the significance of stops and shutter speeds, and providing a series of photographs which help to demonstrate the potentialities of both film and camera.

Films are almost always rated in terms of general sensitivity, since this is the important factor in exposure determination. Until one has acquired personal experience of the performance of a film, one uses the manufacturer's speed rating which appears on every carton.

STANDARD MATERIAL — high speed — (20 — 27 DIN/80 — 400 ASA)

This high speed, under normal lighting conditions, admits of medium stops and fast shutter speeds; this makes for technical reliability and a minimum of exposure problems. Whether, within this group, one decides upon a slower or faster film is dependent upon personal factors.

Films of differing manufacture may, despite bearing the same speed rating, exhibit varying properties, and may also require different developing times. A known, and well tested film should not be abandoned in favour of a new film without first making exhaustive tests.

ULTRA-SPEED FILMS (28 DIN/500 ASA and above)

Special materials for very bad lighting conditions. Make full use of the format! A field for the expert. Interesting effects from the creative potentialities of coarse grain.

VERY LOW SPEED FILMS (14 — 19 DIN/20 — 64 ASA)

Thin emulsion coating and high resolving power permit extreme enlargement. But the exposure latitude is very small, demanding accurate exposure. Also, the low speed entails longer exposure, so beware of camera shake! The use of a tripod will often be of advantage.

DOCUMENT FILMS (7 — 13 DIN/4 — 16 ASA)

These films are still slower, and are characterized by extremely fine grain and high contrast. Development must therefore be adapted to individual circumstances. Their special sphere includes the copying of line originals, yellowed documents, half tone reproduction, landscapes of very low contrast, photography in misty conditions, etc. The results are outstanding, but it is essential, by making a series of tests, first to become thoroughly conversant with exposure and development requirements. For the series, make the first exposure as for 4 DIN/2 ASA, and for each successive exposure shorten it by half a stop, or the equivalent in shutter speed. Suitable development is 5 minutes in Rodinal 1:50, or if still softer negatives are required, 5 minutes in 1:100. The greater the developer dilution, the softer the negative.

Left: photograph taken on a 17 DIN/40 ASA film. Right: infra-red photograph with red filter. The meadow land is reproduced light, because the green colour (chlorophyll) strongly reflects infra-red.

BLACK-AND-WHITE REVERSAL FILM

Useful for all who wish to make reproductions from books, for example as slides for teaching and educational purposes. The purchase price includes the cost of the reversal processing, and the result is a transparency ready for projection. As with all colour reversal films, the exposure latitude is small, which makes accurate exposure essential.

INFRA-RED FILMS

These films are for photography by invisible radiation beyond the visible red (700 — 900 nm, according to make). Since the films are sensitive also to part of the visible light, this has to be eliminated by the use of an infra-red filter. Also the long wave radiation requires a small correction in focus. In general the increase in camera extension needed is 1/22 — 1/300 of the focal length. It is helpful to stop down to f/8 or f/11. The exposure increase factors for the filter differ so widely for the different types of film that for unfamiliar conditions a text exposure is most strongly advised. The application of these films lies mostly in the scientific sphere.

The Kodak false colour Aero-Ektachrome Infra-red film (Type 8443) requires no focusing correction, since only one of the three layers is sensitive to infra-red.

BASIC CONSIDERATIONS FOR CHOICE OF SUBJECT

What should one photograph? All the technical side — from loading the camera to drying the processed film — is something which one can learn and acquire by experience. But just as learning to read music and a few five-finger exercises do not make a pianist, so facility with technique does not in itself get us very far in choice of subject. It is only the beginning. What matters is discrimination in selection from the wealth of visual impression.

As an example, let us suppose that a young amateur photographer is asked by a neighbour one Sunday morning to photograph his very special flower garden. To give an idea of its over-all beauty our friend takes a general view. When they come to examine the result, both the owner and the photographer are equally disappointed. The many thousands of blooms have been bunched up together in a mass of minute spots. Trees and branches have become a tangled confusion. It is a very different matter to "scan" a garden in full bloom with our living eyes, lingering at will on interesting details, as compared with making a single record of the whole mass without discrimination. The aim should be not how much we include to convey the general impression, but how little.

Our speech provides a good parallel. When we speak of a "blond" or a "thickhead" we are making use of one typical characteristic as descriptive of the individual as a whole. This we should likewise do with photography.

So we take a general photograph of the garden for orientation, but then proceed to take close-ups of individual blooms. This could keep us busy with the camera the whole day long, ever and again finding something new and still more beautiful. The owner, however, will be delighted if his favourite bloom appears "full frame" in the resulting series.

This emphasis on subject selection cannot be too greatly stressed. Take an occasional look at a family photograph album. There you will probably find examples of children taken at far too great a distance in a big meadow, the children appearing so small as to be almost unrecognizable. We must learn to visualize our subject as it will later appear in the photograph.

Filling the format is especially important with colour film. With reversal film it is a very complicated business to mask out the superfluous. The same applies to colour negative film: the low price machine processed prints are made from the whole format. Masking and individual treatment becomes expensive. We should take care to choose the optimum framing when we take the photograph.

There is a practical and inexpensive expedient to this end. Take an empty 5 x 5 cm slide frame and hold it in front of the eye at a distance equal to the focal length of the camera lens (e.g. 40 mm), closing the other eye. What is then seen in the frame corresponds to the picture which would appear in the viewfinder. As in the finder, we see all the reference points, the proportion of line and surface within the chosen framing. As compared with the camera viewfinder the slide frame has the advantage that we can have it always with us. By increasing the distance of the frame from the eye to 90 mm, we can see the picture as it would appear with a 90 mm lens. So, even without the camera, we can check which would be the most suitable lens for any particular subject. With this little frame we rapidly learn to apply one of photography's most important rules: Fill the format.

Three things are important to every exposure: the lighting, the viewpoint, and the framing. Their order of importance is indeterminate. We have already discussed framing. Equally important to the composition of a photograph is viewpoint. There are cases where the photographer lies flat on the ground because only from this "worm's eye view" can the desired pictorial effect be achieved. Small children are best photographed from waist level, because normal standing eye-level photographs tend to give a very "looking down on them" impression. If you kneel down to photograph your wife, she will at once appear taller (fashion photography). We should study carefully the changes in perspective which result in the near foreground from even small changes in viewpoint. A few centimetres to right or left, up or down, can be crucial.

Above all other considerations however is the question of lighting. After all, a photograph, a "light picture", is impossible in the absence of light. And of light without shade. Both are fundamentally necessary not only for

On the beach and among the sand dunes we frequently encounter simple subjects like this. The powerful illumination of the light-coloured sand lends itself to contre-jour photography.

the production of a photograph, but also for the composition of a picture. A village fountain, photographed in the morning with the sun behind the camera, may give only an everyday picture, but in the late afternoon — by contre-jour lighting — it may well become a "masterpiece". Shadows can spoil a picture, but on the other hand they can be the making of it. Success here demands practice and experience, for the eye sees things differently from the camera. The eye can embrace light contrasts of 1000:1; photographic paper can reproduce only a range of 30:1. There is no fixed

While on safari in Africa, our bus ran into a mud-hole. The Leica CL is an ideal camera for taking snapshots in such situations.

rule: to every rule there are exceptions which illustrate that occasionally we should take a risk. In this way we learn to appreciate the variety of forms and effects that lighting can achieve.

Line and form

Pictorial effect does not depend only upon content: form plays its part. Obviously we are not bound to any particular format, or printing paper. Any undesirable feature can be masked or cut out.

A picture may be conceived as flat or spatial, with high contrast between light and shade, foreground and background, or quite subdued, with little contrast in tone. Whether the linear distribution — the ornament so to speak — is alone the basis of the composition; whether we concentrate rather on perspective or on light and shade effects, nobody bothers about "rules" in composition: all that matters is the "picture".

84

Picture content

So far as picture content is concerned, there is one rule only: a photograph must have "something to say", in order to constitute a picture. It may, for instance, depict some small occurrence "without frills" (snapshot); it may record an event (Press or reportage); it can produce a purely factual record of some object (technical or product photography); or it can play upon our emotions (sentiment picture). According to the inclination and discernment of the "man behind the camera" his pictures will vary in the nature of their content. The stronger his personality, the more will his photographs bear his "handwriting".

The path of the amateur stems from the photo album, the value of which as a documentation of personal experience nobody would dispute, to culminate ultimately in what one terms a "creative composition". Actually, this path is a form of simplification. By studying good prototypes, in photography or graphic art, we come to appreciate that the degree of perfection achieved is the more, the greater the simplicity of the media employed. The more experience we have of photography, the more we concentrate upon simple subjects. A picture which thus presents the essential, omitting the unimportant, can become meaningful, symbolic.

The part played by lighting

The "light source" in outdoor photography is the sun. Without regard to the wishes of the photographer it follows its path through the sky, hiding behind clouds or shining from a clear sky. In the course of the day, and with the change of the seasons, it presents the world in a thousand different aspects. We have become so completely accustomed to seeing the details of our environment in all these different guises that for the most part we simply no longer appreciate the finer differences in their illumination.

If we take our photography seriously, not restricting our activities to taking souvenir snapshots, we must develop a kind of "feeling" for the finer points of lighting. By careful observation, and from a critical study of photographs which have been failures as a result of unsuitable lighting, we learn that in the morning the appearance of things is different from at midday; under the blazing sun of a summer day different from under the yellow light of winter or the gloom of a rainy day.

Even in the unchanging light conditions of a sunny day the lighting of a subject changes with viewpoint. Viewpoint and lighting are closely interrelated. With the sun behind the camera it gives a frontal illumination to the subject. This type of lighting is occasionally suitable for colour photography, because the differing colours provide sufficient variety. For black-and-white photography it is less suitable, since it yields "flat" pictures with no enlivening shadows, no relief, and no impression of depth.

A simple experiment will clearly demonstrate the effect of changing the illumination of a subject. Look first at a section of cobbled paving with the sun "in your back". Then move slowly in a semi-circle around the selected area, so that it is viewed first in side-lighting and finally with the sun facing you. This will illustrate that side-lighting, and still more back-lighting, brings life to the otherwise dead-looking stone. If, for the purpose of this experiment, we make use of our little slide frame, the effect will be still more clearly demonstrated.

The effects seen on the paving are equally apparent in many subjects in sunlight. Side and back lighting are almost always preferable to frontal lighting. Since, however, there are many things which we are not able, as in the case of the paving, to photograph from any angle we may choose, in most cases there is no alternative but to wait until it pleases the sun to illuminate our subject suitably from the right direction. It can also happen that we have to wait until 4 o'clock in the afternoon to photograph something which we first spotted at 10 o'clock in the morning, simply because we noticed at the time that it would be until then that the lighting would give us the effect we wanted. Even if we cannot wait, because we are only passing through, we need not sacrifice the picture altogether: we can at last take a souvenir snapshot. But we should then always admit to ourselves: It could have been better.

Correct lighting is of special importance in architectural photography. Experts in this field speak of the "crucial half-hour", by which they mean the brief space of time during which the sun comes to shine exactly at glancing incidence across the face of a building. In such lighting even a roughcast wall, traversed by delicate shadows, comes to life.

The ideal "photographic weather" is not sunshine from a clear blue sky. What we need for outdoor photography are great banks of cloud. These act as giant reflectors whose broad shafts of reflected light relieve the shadows and bathe everything in soft lighting. Hazy sunshine, too, provides a pleasing lighting for foreground subjects.

The cobbled road surface has almost disappeared from our towns, but how attractive it looks against the light. Summicron-C f/2, 40 mm, f/11, 1/125 sec.

86

Rain should not disturb us. With the high light transmission of the Summicron f/2, 40 mm we can make hand-held exposures in any weather.

Even if the sun fails altogether to put in an appearance, that is no reason at all for leaving the Leica CL at home. There are thousands of close-up subjects which are worth our attention even in dull weather. And a really soaking wet day! Then the world is literally "swimming" in subjects. We can photograph the umbrella-armed passers-by, with their reflections in the wet road surface, or just the rings around the drops of rain in the puddles. But don't forget the lens hood!

But among the most rewarding photographic experiences is a misty day. Fog is the great master and simplifier of everything. Contrast is almost wiped out, detail disappears, and all that remain are sketchy shapes fading into the grey background of nothingness.

Artificial light photography

Whereas in daylight we can but rarely do anything to influence the

There is something specially attractive about circus photographs. From the front row they are quite easy to take. Here, selective exposure determination is a great advantage.

lighting, artificial light does offer us this facility. Normally the procedure is to start with one main light source and with this try to light our subject in such a manner as to clearly reveal its characteristic features. First we check whether the shadows show the right contrast. Without changing the position of the first lamp, the gradation can be controlled by relieving the shadows by means of a reflector. Such a reflector has the advantage, over the use of a second light source, of delicate control. Recourse is had to a second lamp only after the best possible use has been made of the main light source. This second lamp is used either as a shadow fill light, in which case it must be weaker than the main light, so as not to destroy the original shadows. Alternatively we can use it as an effects light, in which case it may be brighter, but only within limits. It may take the form of a spotlight, with which relatively small areas can be intensely lighted from a considerable distance. In some cases, as a makeshift, the light beam of the slide projector can serve as a spotlight. Since the projection lamp can be used

G

only in its working position, a small mirror is then employed to deflect the light, secured to the projection lens with florist's wire.

Depending upon the form and colour of our subject, the background lighting also plays an important part. In many cases a lamp is used to this end, so adjusted in brightness as to cause the subject to stand out well.

Finally a further tip to those who wish to take portraits at home without going to too much trouble. Replace the existing ceiling lamps by four 100 watt or two 200 watt lamps, in addition switching on any available standard lamps, then move around with the sitter, noting the varying effect of the lighting. There will always be found one position in which a satisfactory effect can be achieved without need for further equipment.

Flash exposures

Flash is one of those artificial light sources whose colour temperature resembles that of daylight. But because its duration is extremely short, so short that it is impossible for the eye to judge its effect, it differs in so many respects from other light sources as to call for a section to itself. To begin with, the equipment needed for flashbulb and for electronic flash is totally different.

The question is — which? At the cold buffet nobody notices it if there is a soft click from the Leica CL (of course without the flash) because everyone's busy choosing. The short focal length of the Summicron f/2, 40 mm still gives adequate sharpness even at full aperture. 1/30 sec ordinary room lighting.

1. FLASHBULBS and FLASH CUBES

Both these types of flash are on the same principle. A highly inflammable metal in an atmosphere of oxygen is contained within a small glass bulb. Ignition is effected by a current surge from a small condenser, and the flashbulb lights up from the resulting explosive combustion — but only once. There is a certain time delay from the ignition point to full brilliance: consequently with the Leica CL flashbulbs cannot be used with all shutter speeds. See Table page 33.

Flash cubes comprise four flashbulbs in a single unit. After the first flash the cube is rotated through 90⁰, bringing the second bulb into position for use. The third and fourth bulbs follow exactly the same procedure. The principal advantages of the flash cube lie in the quick succession of flashes which they permit, and the economy of space. For a considerable time now flashbulbs and flash cubes have been supplied "blue", so that the light emitted may be of the correct colour temperature for "daylight" colour materials.

Equipment for the use of flashbulbs or flash cubes is very small, light, and inexpensive. The batteries, too, which are needed for ignition are cheap and long lasting. The light output of flash bulbs is constant, so that one soon acquires "empirical values" from one's results. Those who only take occasional flash shots, but wish nevertheless to be prepared for them at any time, for example when travelling, would be well advised to buy a small flash cube unit. With 3 flash cubes it weighs about 85 grammes.

2. ELECTRONIC FLASH UNITS

With these units the flash is produced by an electric discharge through a tube filled with a rare gas. Since the gas becomes incandescent only, but is not changed in the process, it can be used again and again. A special advantage lies in the extremely short flash duration. This renders it possible to obtain perfectly sharp records even of subjects in rapid motion. This however also involves the necessity for so choosing the shutter speed of the Leica CL that the shutter blinds are completely free of the entire format when the flash occurs. See table on page 33.

Electronic flash units come large and small, simple and computer controlled. In the latter case the light reflected by the flash-illuminated subject is measured by a built-in sensor, and the flash curtailed when the exposure corresponding to the measurement has been reached. There are

For colour photography the use of flash is frequently advisable. With the centre contact in the accessory shoe of the Leica CL operation is very simple, because with most flash units it is thus unnecessary to use a cable connection. The more recent models, with tilting reflector and automatic flash duration control, are specially to be recommended.

so many flash units that only fundamental considerations can be dealt with here. When first using any flash equipment, the manufacturer's instructions should always be strictly adhered to.

Where flash is frequently used, electronic flash has a number of advantages. The equipment however calls for more careful use and treatment than a simple unit using flashbulbs. The number of flashes an electronic flash unit can give depends upon the state of charge of the accumulator or the type and condition of the battery.

GUIDE NUMBERS

The guide number is a way of expressing the quantity of light which a flash unit is capable of emitting in a single flash. It is used in accordance with the following equation:

$$\frac{\text{Guide number}}{\text{distance}} = \text{stop} \quad \text{or} \quad \frac{\text{Guide number}}{\text{stop}} = \text{distance}$$

It is an average value, based on exposures made in ordinary rooms and for medium distance. The guide number is usually given for a film speed of 21 DIN/100 ASA. The guide number calculation is based on the fact that the intensity of light falls off in proportion to the square of the distance from the light source, and that light transmitted by the lens diaphragm alters in proportion to the square of the stop diameter.

A guide number which is quoted for a film speed of 21 DIN can be adapted to a higher or lower film speed by the use of the following table:

DIN	12	15	18	21	24	27	30
Multiply by	0.35	0.5	0.7	1	1.4	2	2.8

For example, suppose the guide number specified for 21 DIN is 24, then for 27 DIN it must be multiplied by 2 (=48). For a film speed of only 18 DIN the factor is 0.7, giving a guide number of 16.8 (or approximately 17).

The technique of flash

Many flash units are so constructed that they will slip direct into the accessory shoe of the Leica CL. This is certainly very convenient, and for indoor shots is also adequate, but the resulting frontal illumination gives a flat lighting effect. Also, because of the fall-off in intensity of light with increasing distance from the flash, causing the foreground to be much more brightly lighted than the background, this difference becomes very apparent in the resulting photograph. Such photographs are instantly recognizable as flash shots. In this respect, flash lighting can be improved if the flash is directed not at the subject but at the ceiling, so that only diffused reflected light reaches the subject. If the flash unit is not equipped with a tilting facility, a flash reflector can be interposed to the same end. The increased effective working distance, via the ceiling, from flash to main subject reduces the effective illuminating power of the flash, but its effect is to some extent compensated by the fact that the lighting now comes from above and is much more uniform throughout the depth of the subject. For "bounce" flash, as this is termed, the height of the room should not exceed 2.6 metres, as otherwise the loss of light will be too great. In calculating the guide number the distance is taken as "camera — ceiling — subject". In practice this means that for close work (2 metres) the lens will have to be opened up by 2 stops as compared with direct flash. At greater distances (3 — 5 metres) about 1 stop will suffice.

Should we wish to use the flash off the camera, by means of a cable connector, a small adapter is available for the centre contact of the Leica CL. We can then, by means of a shorter or longer connector, freely use the flash in any desired position. Here a word of advice: Hold the flash unit high up with the left hand, with the index finger so placed that we can sense with it the direction in which the flash is pointed. This control is always

Flash can be a great help in child photography. In most cases indirect (bounce) flash (up to a ceiling height of about 2.6 metres) can be used. It gives more uniform lighting, because there is much less light fall-off towards the background.

important in using direct flash. Also, if someone else is holding the flash, it is necessary that they should adjust the flash direction to suit the field of view embraced by the lens in use. When side lighting is used, some adjustment (½ — 1 stop) should be made to compensate for light loss.

Flash is not recommended for rooms where there is noticeable smoke. Smoke scatters the light in the same way that car headlight beams are scattered by fog. The resulting pictures are flat and lacking in contrast, particularly when the flash has to be used on the camera.

There are many situations in which flash and daylight combined can yield outstanding results. Over-deep shadows can be relieved, or the flash be used as substitute for non-existent sunlight. At short distances, flash is actually brighter than sunlight. There is, however one thing to watch.

Witches' carnival at Offenburg. For outdoor flash shots the guide number is lower than the normal rating (e.g. 18 instead of 28), because there is no reflection from walls, ceiling.

When flash is used as a substitute for sunlight, it must be about four times as intense as the prevailing daylight. The only shutter speeds permissible are 1/60 sec and slower (on account of synchronization requirements). The flash illumination is calculated from the guide number, the daylight intensity from the selective exposure measurement with the Leica CL. If the shutter speed is slowed to 1/30 sec, the daylight contribution is doubled; at 1/15 sec quadrupled, and in that case a tripod will be needed. The relationship is not altered by any change of stop. Outdoors, the daylight contribution remains constant at all distances; the flash intensity however falls off rapidly with the distance.

If flash is used to lighten the shadows, which can be very useful outdoors in contre-jour shots, here, too, 1/60 sec is the fastest permissible shutter speed. The very deep shadows are ignored in determining the exposure.

The guide number is doubled in calculating, thus limiting the flash range. Should the flash then still be too bright, because of a comparatively short working distance, its intensity should be reduced by interposing a sheet of vellum paper, or one or two pocket handkerchiefs. With computer flash units slight underexposure will result, that is, a lightening of the shadows, if the film speed is set higher (3-5 DIN/1.5 — 2.5 ASA).

When first experimenting in this field, a number of exposures should be made, successively differing by one stop, in order to gain experience. Exposure data should be noted down.

Practice films

If we but rarely use it, the Leica CL remains a stranger to us: much about it may seem complicated and difficult, because we have to think what we are doing at every trick and turn. To make any progress in the direction of rapid and reliable operation demands practice. Using the camera unloaded, to start with: it's cheaper — but there will be no results to compare.

However, black-and-white miniature films are so cheap that we should not lightly sacrifice the advantages that the taking of an actual negative offers. The film need only be developed, and when dry can be critically examined. The 40 mm Summicron can itself be taken out of the camera if need be and used as a magnifier. It gives a x6 magnification, and of course has first class definition. But take care, in looking closely through it, not to soil the lens surface.

Strictly speaking, a better way is to cut up the practice film and mount the individual negatives in 5 x 5 cm interchangeable (glass) mounts, projecting them with a miniature projector. On a 1 metre wide screen every little defect will become instantly apparent, such as would not even be detectable on a 7 x 10 cm paper print. Since in this way we avoid the making of prints, the negatives being taken out of the slide mounts and these used again and again, the whole exercise is very inexpensive. It is only these negatives, by the way, that need be thus cut up into individual frames: ordinary negatives are normally cut into strips of six frames, which are convenient for filing.

What to photograph in this practice film? There can be no rigid rules, since previous experience will differ in individual cases. Complete beginners will start right at the beginning, with loading and unloading the film in the camera. Then practice pressing the release, with the camera in both

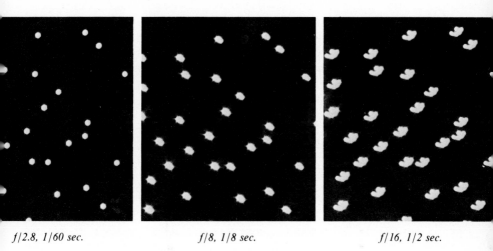

f/2.8, 1/60 sec.   *f/8, 1/8 sec.*   *f/16, 1/2 sec.*

horizontal and vertical format position, without shaking the camera. As a check on this, photograph a sheet of dark paper, about 40 x 60 cm in size, in which a dozen holes have been punched with a pin. The paper should be fixed to a window in such a position that the light shines through the holes. The photograph should be taken at the shortest focusing distance (0.8 metre with 40 mm lens, 1 metre with 90 mm lens) and the first photograph taken at f/16 with ¼ sec. Stop and shutter speed are then altered a stop at a time until f/2.8 is reached, at 1/125 sec. Here again the negatives are checked with the magnifier. The slowest shutter speed of ¼ sec will usually show a certain amount of movement blur. From the negatives taken with the large apertures, and consequently faster shutter speeds, it can also be checked whether the focusing has been accurate. As consolation it may be mentioned that even experienced photographers sometimes get movement blur with 1/30 sec.

Focusing is important. Since most of the things we shall photograph have spatial depth, i.e. individual features extend to differing distances from the camera, in the case of the somewhat longer distances *estimation* of distance may be both better and quicker; however in order to arrive at a correct decision we have to know what is the depth of field at medium stops for medium distances. To this end we once again take some test pictures, at distances of 3, 5, and 10 metres. Suitable subjects are market scenes including foreground features, street scenes with cars and pedestrians. A glance at the scale will tell us how far the depth of field extends into foreground and background. On travel, particularly, this is important, for speed of operation is much greater if we are familiar with these things. In the close-up range, that is to say at less than 2 metres distance, it is usually best to measure the distance accurately, and this is something which perhaps we should practise more frequently. Thus we can take comparison photographs of, for example, a fountain figure, from different distances. This will assist us in judging how close to approach to make best use of the format.

For the more experienced, one field of experiment is the movement study. In the viewfinder we watch people passing by, noting the distance and the manner of their walking. To ourselves we count, left. . .right. . . and press the release when, as we may think fit, the left or the right foot "touches down". That is not to say that people should only be photographed in this position, but we should learn how, if we want to record a particular position, to be sure of achieving it.

At the fountain. Just an example of practice shots. From this we can learn how flowing water can change in appearance at different shutter speeds.

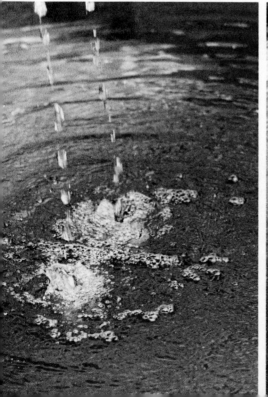
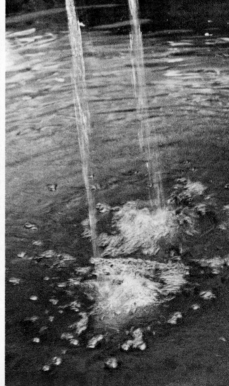

Swinging on the beach. Since the movement is continually repeated I could choose my own moment to press the release. I met these two children singing as they walked near Fiss in the Tirol.

A much more difficult situation is when the subject is approaching us, because we have then simultaneously to correlate distance, format utilization, and foot position. The distance can be set in advance, and the release pressed when the subject has reached this predetermined position. The correct distance will have been reached when the subject is the right size in the finder. But still we have to watch that he is also "in step".

To really get the hang of this technique, we can make a few dozen exposures at our leisure: it will then be not quite such a big step from simple walking to sports photography. Here again the crucial factor is pressing the release just at the correct phase. To take good sports photographs, however, it is not enough to know something of photography: one must also have some technical knowledge of the particular sport in question.

Snapshot technique

"That would make a first class snapshot". Every photographic old-timer will have experienced such situations. But to turn wanting into getting calls for some experience.

The first essential is the correct manipulation of the camera (further details in the section "Practice films") so that we are always ready with our Leica CL at a moment's notice. Operation is rendered all the faster the more it can be simplified. Normally, in taking any photograph three variables have to be set: distance, stop, and shutter speed. Quite apart from actually making an exposure we can set stop and shutter speed for the prevailing light conditions. So long as these do not change, all we then have to do is to focus for the particular situation. If a 35, 40, or 50 mm focus lens is used, it is sufficient in many cases to estimate the distance, but in using the 90 mm it is safer to measure it.

Should we wish to remain unobserved up to the very last moment, the best way is to focus, not on the actual subject, but on some other object which is at the same distance but in another direction. Collating distances in this way is a measure of our ability to estimate distance. We watch our subject, and at the right moment raise the Leica CL to the eye and immediately press the release. Here it is almost always helpful if our "photographic reaction time" is such that the situation doesn't change meanwhile.

The best shutter speeds are 1/125 to 1/500 sec. It is better to use a fast shutter speed and correspondingly larger stop, because extra depth of field is of no use if the definition is spoilt by movement blur.

Where it is desired to take a picture completely unobserved, as can be useful in the Far East or in Africa, "blind" shooting can be adopted, i.e. shooting without looking through the finder. For example the Leica CL can be carried on the chest with the camera strap, aimed by reference to the lens, and the shutter released preferably with a 50 cm cable release operated from the pocket without actually looking at the subject. Shutter speed, stop, and distance are set in advance, using some other subject which is not in the same sense "critical". The technique, and familiarity with how much can be included in the format with a 35, 40, or 50 mm lens should have been practised at home beforehand. Here, the following, very much simplified, formula may help: Select some object at a distance of 100 fl (focal lengths); this will give an image 1/100th of the actual size, and the subject area covered will be 2.4 x 3.6 metres. With a 50 mm lens the distance will thus be 5 metres, with a 40 mm lens 4 metres, or with a 35 mm

Anyone who visits Antwerp should not fail to visit the Rubens House: it is well worth while. Needless to say there are ready made postcards there for sale, but to take one's own photographs is much more satisfying, and they carry more personal recollections. Summicron-C 40 mm, f/2.8, 1/30 sec.

lens 3.5 metres. This last focal length has a special advantage: the distance corresponds to the width of the film, because the width of the negative format, 36 mm, is almost exactly the same as the 35 mm focal length. It is comparatively easy to aim the lens at the middle of the subject and estimate the distance with the eyes on the ground. It is rarely that one is suspected of taking photographs with the camera not held up to the eye.

Snapshots are not always concerned with rapid movement. Their importance lies in providing a typical and characteristic impression of a whole situation. Occasionally a certain amount of "direction" may be brought in to help, but then it is no longer a snapshot.

Travel

A trip away from home, whether just in the surrounding country or abroad, always gains in interest by suitable preparation. Naturally it is a pleasant experience to come across something beautiful which we had not expected; but many things worth seeing are somewhat hidden away, and it would have been a pity to have missed them. There are often so many things worth seeing that only a few of them can really leave a lasting memory. If we are to exercise discrimination in making our photographic records, the following rules should become quite automatic as part of our normal viewing of a scene. First of all we take a general look, embracing the whole scene, only then passing to a more lingering examination of the specially interesting features. Applied to the photographic aspect, this means taking a general view with the Summicron-C 40 mm followed by closer looks at the interesting features with the Elmar-C 90 mm. If we have no 90 mm lens, then we must approach to a nearer viewpoint until we include the same area in the picture; this may even mean using the shortest working distance of 80 cm. Then, back home, we can at our leisure study our records more closely and relive our experiences. Frequently we shall discover interesting details which at the time passed unobserved, simply because there was so much to see.

Colour photography represents more than 80% of the whole, so in the following tips we have primarily colour film in mind. In order, on a longish trip, to ensure that all our colour photographs shall have the same general colour characteristics, we should take with us only films not merely of the same make and type, but also as far as possible of the same emulsion number. Before starting out, tests should be made on a film of this type so that we know exactly what its characteristics are. Prior to setting out, the films should have been stored in a refrigerator — and this also applies to any which are still left after return — because cool storage assists the keeping quality of the film. The films should be sent for processing immediately on return, since they are liable to deteriorate if kept unprocessed for any length of time.

Landscapes

Landscapes are more difficult to photograph than the beginner might suppose. His instinctive preference is for the wide view — getting as much as possible in one picture — but typical selective views are usually more effective. There are no general rules for procedure, but a few hints as to what one should not do may be helpful. In seascapes the horizon must not

A fence in the foreground helps to give the effect of depth. For years past such subjects have been popular in colour.

102

be tilted through tilting of the camera, and the horizon moreover should not run right through the middle of the picture. Sunsets are not worth while in black-and-white, and even in colour they present difficulties.

For photographs in which there is a large expanse of sky with extensive cloud effects a short focus lens (35 or 40 mm) is the best to use.

The same is true of a narrow valley. But in many cases a 90 mm lens is better, because while its narrow angle records less of the subject, it records it on a larger scale. More variety than is offered in flat country is to be found in mountainous and Alpine regions. But the best picture is not always the view from the topmost peak. From such a height the neighbouring mountains look little more than hillocks. Such a view gives no idea of the vastness of the surrounding scene which dominates the visual impression. A suitable foreground — with a somewhat longer focal length — is more effective. Still greater possibilities — if we don't mind facing the climbing involved — are usually offered by a viewpoint some hundreds of metres short of the peak, from which the immensity of the mountain is more impressive.

Lighting — in most cases the sun's position — plays an important role. Midday, with the sun at its highest point is less suitable than the more oblique lighting, earlier or later, with its longer shadows.

Delicate effects and gradations can be achieved by including some strong accents in the foreground. Paths and other lines leading into the picture help to give spatial effect to the subject.

Lake scenes in snow can be fascinating in contre-jour lighting, but great care must be taken that no direct sunlight enters the lens. In some cases the lens hood is not long enough, especially with a low sun. A glance through the finder will reveal the sun in the lower right hand corner. The intensity of the direct sunlight is so great that it will give rise to reflections within the lens which distribute themselves over the picture and render it useless. This trouble, moreover, is especially to be found with high grade wide aperture lenses with many components and steep curvatures. General fogging, to, can result from any contamination of the front or back lens, even a heavy finger-print.

ARCHITECTURAL PHOTOGRAPHS

These can form an important part of one's photography when travelling, for example, in Italy or France. Apart from the general requirements of

This beautiful fishpond is in a building adjoining Kremsmunster monastry (Upper Austria). Summicron-C f/2.8, f/2, 40 mm, f/8, 1/125 sec.

lighting — frontal, side, or diffused light on a cloudy day — an overriding consideration is the choice of a suitable focal length to embrace the whole building. The longer focal lengths are in general preferable, but in most cases one is restricted by having to work in narrow alleys or other confined spaces, where only a wide angle lens is any use. If we have then to photograph the building from the street, it will be possible to include the whole building in the picture only by tilting the camera, which will result in converging verticals; for the vertical lines of a building will appear vertical on the photograph only if the film plane of the camera was vertical when the picture was taken. This can be checked, if a tripod is used, by looking at the camera from a distance of about 1½ metres in front of and to one side of it, to ensure that the horizontal and vertical setting of the camera agree with the corresponding lines of the subject.

Oblique upward view of the Parthenon on the Acropolis in Athens. Elmarit f/2.8, 28 mm, f/8, 1/60 sec, orange filter, 40 ASA film.

Since, however, most photographs will be taken with the camera hand held, we shall not usually notice from the outset whether there is in fact any up or down tilt to it. This can be checked by looking at the edge of the viewfinder field. In some cases it is possible to photograph a building from an upper floor of a building opposite, thereby avoiding the need for any camera tilt. Provided the necessary equipment is available, converging verticals can, within limits, be corrected in enlarging. This however becomes fairly expensive if done professionally.

Here, as in many other recommendations, there are exceptions. Slightly converging verticals are most disturbing when we have the conscious feeling that they ought to be vertical. On the other hand if we tilt the camera to such an extent that one realises that the convergence is

Basel cathedral is a building of art historical interest. These early sculptures in the porch are noteworthy. The Elmarit-C f/4, 90 mm in this case gave a more successful picture because it is permitted a more distant viewpoint, thereby entailing less camera tilt.

deliberate, it can add to the effect of the picture, as our example shows. In this picture of the Parthenon on the Athens Acropolis the Leica CL was tilted steeply upwards. The lens used was an Elmarit f/2.8, 28 mm. It was one of the new type with serial numbers above 2314922 (Note: the older type cannot be used with the Leica CL because it projects too deeply into the camera body). To make the brilliant white marble stand out strongly against the blue sky, an orange filter was used. This increased the exposure required by four times, but in the brilliant lighting of the southern sun this presented no difficulty. Unfortunately there was nothing which could be included in the photograph to give an idea of dimensions, so that it is not apparent how enormous are these columns. For such a subject a wide angle lens is not essential. There is sufficient space to allow of taking a normal picture from a longer distance, using a somewhat longer focus lens.

Very beautiful renaissance and baroque furniture is to be seen in the Papuis Palace in Wetzlar. This forms part of the well known Lemmers-Danforth collection.

Many buildings are especially "photogenic" with a particular position of the sun. If time permits, it is worth waiting for this "quarter-hour". Apart from the general view, detail pictures are worth taking, to round off and supplement the general view.

Interior photographs

The brightness of the interiors of churches and museums plays a decisive role when photographing them. There are many possibilities of taking photographs even in these places, if a highly sensitive colour film (160 ASA) is used, as the speed of the latter can be increased to as much as 400 ASA by special processing. We should have a thorough knowledge of the material we are using and therefore it is highly advisable to expose a test film before starting off on an important journey. The exposure time is best measured at full aperture. If we have to stop down a great deal because we need to get great depth of field, then the reciprocity failure effect becomes

Always be at the ready when photographing village scenes. This photograph was taken from a distance of some 30 feet. Data: 1/250 sec. at f/8, 120 ASA film.

apparent. For instance, if our measurement gives us 1/30 sec. at f/2 and we wish to use f/11, then according to the relative aperture of the lens, the exposure would have to be 1 second: making allowance for an increase of 100 percent in order to compensate for reciprocity failure. Two seconds would, however, be the correct exposure. Moreover a slight shift in the colours may be noticed, but as this does not occur to the same extent with all colour films, application should be made to the film manufacturer for information on this point.

Street scenes and portraiture

Foreign countries provide a welcome enrichment to our photographic programme. An abundance of pictorial subjects is to be found in exotic lands. Close-up pictures of natives are particularly interesting. If, however, without knowing the customs and laws of the land, we pull out our camera, we may find ourselves in a very dangerous position. Great care has to be exercised particularly in Islamic countries because in these regions photography is generally unwelcome for religious reasons. Even the photographing of ordinary street scenes is often regarded as a nuisance.

If we have purchased the right to photograph individuals by presenting them with a coin, then the situation is not nearly as unfavourable as it might appear to be at first sight, because we then save ourselves from other troubles. Unfortunately many models stand so stiffly in front of the camera as to make it hardly worth while taking a photograph. It is then a good idea to get a second person to talk to the "victim" in order to detract his or her attention.

Family celebrations

At a christening, first communion or confirmation, on a birthday, or other anniversaries, we get together with friends and relatives in order to celebrate the festive occasion. We like to remember such happy hours and often wish to have a photographic record of them. Such photographs can be taken out of doors in daylight without any difficulty. The rooms in a house vary a great deal in brightness. Many people believe that in this case good pictures can only be obtained by using flash. One certainly obtains pictures in this way, but they are usually practically lifeless and lacking in atmosphere. For colour photographs the flash technique is however indispensable. The particular points to note are to be found on page 91.

If, on the other hand, we are content with black-and-white photographs, then in most cases the ordinary interior illumination will be sufficient if we use a film of maximum sensitivity, 400 ASA. This film is about 5 times as fast as a colour negative film for making colour prints on paper. When used in conjunction with the Summicron-C f/2 40 mm lens we can take photographs on many occasions: in doing so we measure the areas in the face, because these areas are important, and have to put up with the fact that something in the background will be underexposed.

If you develop the film yourself, the speed of the film can be taken as 800 ASA. Use fresh developer always and increase processing time by 30%, or raise the temperature of development by 3°C, but then the entire film should be given a correspondingly brief exposure. This will result in very natural photographs because most of the people present are doubtful if anything will come of it and many of them are even unaware that photographs are being taken because the shutter of the Leica CL is so silent that it can hardly be heard.

Photographs like these of celebrations in the home can be taken almost unnoticed by dispensing with flash and using a really fast film having a speed of 400 ASA. The depth of field is adequate at f/2.8, 1/30 sec. was given.

Wedding photographs

A family chronicle should start with wedding photographs. However, at one's own wedding there is very little opportunity to take photographs and therefore these tips are really intended for the good friends of the bride and bridegroom. The bride and bridegroom will certainly be pleased to have a photo album showing pictures of all the festive proceedings. Since the lighting conditions are sometimes unfavourable for taking indoor photographs, the Leica CL with its controlled exposure measurement presents many advantages. If we only take black-and-white photographs we can manage without flash light. We can use a very fast 400 ASA film, which is adequate for an exposure of 1/30 sec at f/2 in most of the rooms in a house. Let us start off by taking photographs in the registry office. We make just one measurement in a typical place and use the same exposure for all the photographs, otherwise we shall not be quick enough when it

comes to taking immediate action. Having recorded the signing of the register, we now follow this up by taking a photograph of a small group including the bride and bridegroom and the witnesses to the marriage.

One likes to take photographs in the church during the wedding ceremony, but this is not possible without first consulting the minister; it is tactful to ask his permission beforehand. In most cases the necessary permission will be given if we also mention that we will not use flash light and will give proper consideration to the dignity of the proceedings. We should also avoid constantly running about in the church in search of the best positions.

There are occasions when permission is only granted to photograph the arrival and departure of the bride and bridegroom because one's predecessors have been somewhat too impetuous. If the church possesses bright windows, then in many cases we can even take colour photographs at $f/2$. Since we are not using flash the atmosphere is exactly the same as when seen with our eyes.

One of the most impressive photographs is that of the return from the altar to the exit of the church. However, a photograph can only be taken if sufficient light is available. It is less difficult to take photographs in front of the church portal. One can arrange for the bride and bridegroom to remain there for a short time to enable several photographs to be taken. If there are some steps leading down from the portal it is even possible to take a group photograph of the entire wedding company. This must, however, have been arranged previously, otherwise it will take too long to group the people. A few shots of the inquisitive onlookers standing about should also be incidentally recorded. They make a popular addition to a wedding album. Our small amount of reporting should not compete with the usual wedding photographs taken by a professional photographer. He is experienced in the art and will take care to record not only the dress and headdress of the bride, but also the fine detail in them. There still remains enough for us to do if we are to capture all the joyful scenes at a late hour. Even in this case it is a good thing to use films of maximum sensitivity. There is not much point in using flash in rooms in which there is a great deal of smoking, because in a short space of time the air becomes so dense with smoke that the flash light is scattered diffusely and the pictures turn out flat.

Don't economize on film when taking wedding photographs: shoot as if you were a reporter. It gives you the opportunity to prove that you are in full control of your Leica CL.

Grandfather in front of the camera

Many people do not like going to a photographer. When a death occurs it is not unusual to find with regret that no reasonable photograph is available. There are many reasons for being shy of the camera. There are races of men for whom photography is absolutely taboo. In our case it is rather the fear of being photographed to disadvantage, however in the hands of a good professional photographer there is no need to have such qualms as he is well practised in the art of photography. Nevertheless older people no longer wish to go to him and then we have no option but to photograph them in their homes. The set-up of the illumination is the same as that described for the photography of children. As it is also a matter of practice, the first time, we use a very patient person as a test model and seat him on a stool, say in the last third of the row of windows. The use of a stool is important because in the ordinary way we lean against the back of a chair and draw in our chin, and this makes the neck look thicker than necessary. A person sits in a half-inclined position on a stool but with his weight slightly forward. The sitter may find it more comfortable to rest his arm on his knee. In this position the neck will be reproduced slightly tensed but without any wrinkles. Since the light comes from the side, the eyes are not dazzled by it and are thus wide open. For those who wear them there are even fewer reflections from their spectacles and these reflections can more easily be reduced by slightly turning the head, than would be possible out-of-doors.

It is best to sit down on a chair with the camera at a distance of say 6 to 9 feet: with medium speed films we shall still be able to take instantaneous shots at $f/4$. It is advisable to use a somewhat longer focal length, e.g. 90 mm, because we cannot come up close to our model and at the same time fill the image frame. We should also pay attention to the background. It should be as tranquil as possible and not too near. In many cases it would be best first to pretend making some ten exposures (without of course moving on the film). This relaxes the photographer as well as the model. Since, however, our miniature film is not expensive, we can start immediately with the film and later look for any change in relaxation in the

Apart from the way described in the text, there are often excellent opportunities of obtaining good shots of people in every-day situations. If we have a feeling for the effect of light, the rest is only a question of being able to handle the camera quickly. The photograph (lower right) was taken in room lit by its ordinary electric lights and using 400 ASA film.

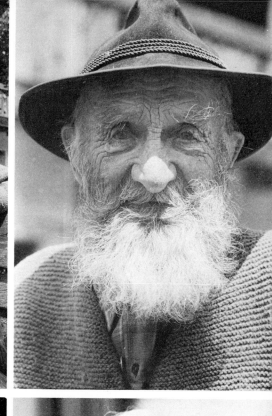

sitter. In many cases a third exposure is a useful means of diverting the attention of a sitter. Our illumination is very suitable for making a portrait showing three quarters of the face. An example of this posture is to be found on German bank notes, all of which show the reproduction of some old master. At the same time we can take note of the disposition of the lines of shadows on the face. Light coming semi-obliquely from the right or left renders the face somewhat thinner, an effect which usually pleases the sitter.

Photography of children in the rooms in a house

Pictures of children are popular. It is by no means difficult to take photographs in a dwelling when the children are playing in their accustomed surroundings. They forget that they are being photographed. It is certainly more convenient to take the photographs out-of-doors because it is brighter there, but in sunshine hard shadows often occur and the children screw up their eyes. In a room it is much easier to arrange the illumination so as not to dazzle their eyes. When the children look into darkness, the pupils of their eyes remain wide open.

If you wish to take the photographs by daylight only, then this is best done in a room with large windows and with the curtains pushed back. To provide suitable lighting conditions set up your projection screen parallel to and at a distance of about five feet from the windows, or, as a makeshift, we hang up a line with a large white cloth attached to it. The small space thus provided is our studio. If possible, arrange for the light to fall from the window on the left and from the reflecting screen on the right. Seat the child or children at a small table so that they can play. This leaves you in peace to focus accurately. The time of exposure will have been measured previously by using a piece of medium grey paper or another person, instead of the children. In many cases the light is sufficiently bright to permit an exposure of 1/30 sec at f/4 to be made (with 80 ASA colour negative film). If you possess a 90 mm lens you should use it, especially when photographing only one child. In order to obtain completely natural pictures, a second person should be there to look after the child or children. This assistance is almost indispensable when there are several children; it is important to distract their attention from being

Photographing children indoors will prove whether we are really capable of handling our CL Leica with the same degree of certainty as a reporter. The exposure to be given must be determined beforehand. The shutter speed and the lens stop having been set it remains only to focus the lens before releasing the shutter.

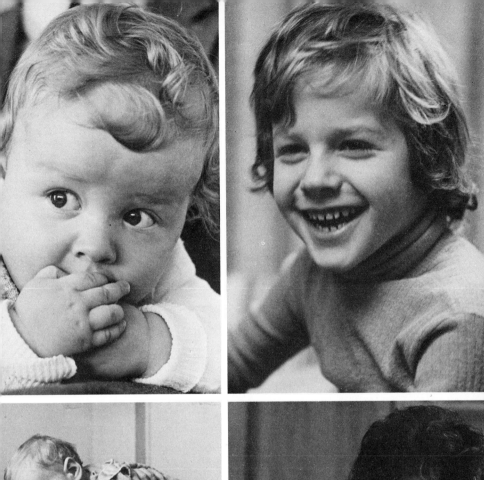

photographed and thus make them appear quite natural and unconstrained. The assistant should be placed near the window so that the children look in the right direction for the illumination. You should place yourself about on a level with the heads of the children: it is not a good thing to photograph children from above.

Patience is needed and a feeling for the right moment. Don't economize on film: you can always select the best pictures afterwards from a series of photographs.

We can also take photographs without daylight, and without going to the previously described trouble, by increasing the normal illumination in the room by means of three or four 100 W incandescent lamps. When used with black-and-white film of maximum speed (400 ASA) it is possible, without further ceremony, to make exposures of 1/30 sec, or less at f/2. A white ceiling is a good scatterer of light and there are many places in a room where harmoniously and well-lighted photographs can be taken. Even ordinary table and standard lamps should be included when studying the illumination. It is important to judge the effect so obtained before making the exposure.

The situation is much more difficult when we want to employ the very bright photographic bulbs — floods — used for cine filming. They emit intense beams of light whereas the ceiling and walls reflect less light resulting in great differences in the dark and light parts of the object photographed. Children are dazzled by the light and screw up their eyes. However, in many cases "indirect" light from the ceiling and walls can be used.

The third and last possiblitiy is to take flash photographs, this can also be done in conjunction with daylight. Since, however, the effect of the flash light cannot be seen and therefore cannot be judged quantitatively, some experience is required to handle it correctly. The advice on flashlight (page 91) tells how to achieve useful results with electronic flash or flash bulbs.

"A photographic archive" of valuable objects

One of the tasks often planned but seldom carried out is that of making a photographic inventory of households possessions or of a collection. When carpets, valuable pictures, antiques or other works of art are stolen, the actual appearance of the stolen goods can often only be inadequately described. Good photographs would be of material assistance to the police in their investigations. Only a general indication can be given here of the

118

It is always advisable to possess a photographic record of valuable old furniture. If the first attempt is not quite successful, the second one may be.

methods to be used for photographing different objects because the conditions vary too greatly. First of all we need a stable tripod because larger objects such as furniture also have to be given "time exposures", even with room illumination.

First inspect the piece of furniture to be photographed from all sides in order to ascertain its characteristic features. The position from which we take the photograph is of paramount importance. The back of the camera must be vertical to the floor to avoid getting any converging lines. In order to show up definite surface structures get somebody to illuminate the object from the side with a portable lamp (100 or 200 watt). When a photograph is taken later on the lamp can be moved during a fairly long exposure: this gives softer and more even illumination. Since the measurement is made from behind the lens, our exposure meter will only give a reading at f/2 when poor lighting conditions prevail. We then base

119

The old oak chest is nearly 300 years old and the wood has acquired a saturated dark tone which, when the time of exposure is measured with the Leica CL camera, yields a somewhat high value. It is advisable to stop down half a stop for black-and-white photographs and it is important to do so when using reversal colour film.

our calculations on f/8. In this case should the times of exposure amount to several seconds we then have to double or even treble the exposure on account of reciprocity failure.

Films of maximum sensitivity shorten the time of exposure but are not necessary when a tripod is used, and in this case it is better to use films of medium to low speed (32 — 125 ASA). The exposure conditions are similar for colour films (50 — 80 ASA).

Some objects, such as paintings, or carpets, really call for colour film. Anyone who wishes to gain experience by making a couple of tests should start off by using colour reversal film with which it is comparatively easy to take photographs out-of-doors in daylight. Direct sunlight is suitable for photographing carpets. But how can we find a suitable position? The lens has to be at the point of intersection of the diagonals, but at a suitable distance — so as to obtain photographs without any distortion. Fairly

Reproduction of a copper engraving by A. Durer: 105 x 148 mm / 4¹/₈ x 5³/₄ in. by daylight at the window — illuminated by white cards. The fourth leg which cast a shadow was removed and the apparatus stabilized by screwing a ball-and-socket joint into the Leica CL camera.

small pieces and rugs can be held by two people in a garden. Since most of them are symmetrical in shape it is often sufficient, when dealing with large pieces, to take in two-thirds of the area of a carpet which is suspended on a curtain rod.

Colour photographs can only be taken indoors if the "colour temperature" is uniform. Flash light is suitable for supplementing the available daylight. You will find more detailed instructions in the section on flashlight. Without daylight we can obtain good photographs with artificial-light colour reversal films by using 2 to 3 photographic bulbs. The position of the bulbs should be such that they illuminate the entire surface of the object and produce a three-dimensional effect without too much contrast. An important part is played by the light reflected by reflecting screens or from the walls. If photographs are taken subsequently using colour negative film in order to obtain colour prints, a grey or colour scale should be photographed at the same time in the case of important objects to act as a guide for the printing establishment for controlling the colours. These wedges and charts are supplied to photographic dealers by the film factories.

Method of photographing a television screen

It is not at all difficult to photograph a television screen if it is remembered that the pictures on the screen of a television set are recorded by a succession of lines. There are 25 images per second and each image consists of 625 lines (2 x 312.5). This takes place so rapidly that we see the picture without any interruptions, due to the inertia of the eye. The camera however cannot be deceived. If we give too short an exposure then only parts of the image can be seen. The shortest time of exposure is therefore 1/30 sec, irrespective of whether we are recording the rapid events in a sports scene or the text of a cookery recipe. Somewhat longer times are possible: with a tripod we can, if necessary, expose for 1/15 or 1/8 sec. The Leica CL camera must be placed in a position such that the lens is on a level with the centre of the screen (intersection of the diagonals). The back of the camera is placed parallel to the television screen. If we are photographing a 60 cm. screen, the distance should be 85 — 90 cm with a 40 mm lens, and about 1.80 — 1.90 m. with a 90 mm lens. The picture is focused by holding a newspaper in front of the viewing screen. The exposure time has already been mentioned. We now have to determine what stop to use by aiming at a point of medium brightness on the screen. Since only pictures of good

Photographs of a television screen serve as a very useful aid to memory.

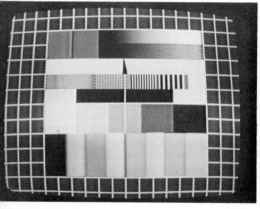 

gradation are suitable for photographing it is important to adjust the television set so as to obtain a bright picture of medium contrast. When using colour reversal film it must be the daylight type. The colours in colour negative films can be influenced during the printing process. The room must be darkened completely, otherwise troublesome reflections may occur on the viewing screen. The photographs thus obtained are for your personal use only; you have no copyright in them.

Close-up photography

With 40 mm lens of the Leica CL camera the nearest we can get to an object is 80 cm: at this distance an area of 40 x 60 cm will be reproduced, corresponding to an image scale of 1:18. At a distance of 1 metre an area of about 20 x 30 cm will be reproduced with a 90 mm lens: an image scale of 1:9. Since we can obtain the same area of the object by using different focal lengths at different distances, the image scale will be given as a reference number in the case of close-ups.

WHAT DOES THE IMAGE SCALE INDICATE?

It indicates the relation (reduction or enlargement) between the sizes of the object and the image reproduced in the film. Example: The size of our photograph is 24 x 36 mm and that of the photographic object is 120 x 180 mm : an image of 1:5 is formed, signifying a reduction to $^1/_{25}$ of the size of the original object. The image scale is 1:5 which can also be written as $1/5 = 0.5$. The decimal form makes it easier to calculate the multiplication factor for the exposure time. This is however immaterial in the case of the Leica CL camera because, by making the measurement behind the lens, allowance is automatically made for the multiplication factors. If the reading is 5:1 this means that the object has been enlarged five times in the reproduction, but as the original is only 4.8 x 7.2 mm in size, in this case the photograph must have been taken through a magnifying glass and it is therefore a macrograph.

HOW CAN WE ACHIEVE A SHARP IMAGE AT CLOSE RANGE?

Distances of less than 00 (infinity) are focused by rotating the helical thread of the lens, and here the coupled rangefinder comes in useful. We increase the distance between the lens and the plane of the film. By how much? The increase corresponds to the image scale. Let us take an example: our objects do not always fit exactly into the ratio aspect of the film. If we wish to photograph a drawing of 18 x 30 cm. in format, the object in this case is narrow its length is then the decisive factor. In the case of wide texts we base our calculation on the width of the film. How often is 300 mm divisible by 36 mm? Here fractions are unimportant, so we always round off the figure to the next higher number, 8 x 36 = 288 mm, 9 x 36 = 324 mm; this is sufficient, and we choose an image scale of 1:9. To obtain a sharp image we need an extension corresponding to the image scale, in our case 1/9 of the focal length. Since the helical thread of the 90 mm Elmar C lens increases in steps of 10 mm we can take the photograph without using any additional device. If, however, we want to make an enlargement on the film of say 3:1, then we shall need an additional extension of 3 focal lengths. Whether we are able to focus a close-up sharply on a given scale depends on whether the necessary extension can be achieved directly with the helical thread or whether it has to be done by using accessories. It is desirable to test the sharpness of the focusing and to see the area of the image formed. Mirror reflex devices are particularly suitable for this purpose.

The Leica CL camera is eminently suitable for travel photography and for reporting, but for extreme close-up work the Leicaflex camera enables us to achieve our object more quickly. However, anyone who possesses these accessories of the Leica system which are suitable for close-up photography will find more detailed instructions of the combination to use on the following pages. The first two instruments are only suitable for 50 mm. lenses.

CLOSE-UP DEVICE DIN A 4 = 210 x 297 mm/8¼ x 11⅝ in.

DIN A 5 = 148 x 210 mm/5¾ x 8¼ in.

(16526)   DIN A 6 = 105 x 148 mm/4⅛ x 5¾ in.

The close-up equipment consists of three intermediate lens pieces and four telescopic metal legs. The intermediate piece is chosen according to the format desired and the four legs are then screwed in and extended as far as the catches which are specified for the format. After having clicked them into place at the respective number, the milled screw cap is easily put on. The points frame the area of the object and at the same time give the distance. The equipment can be used for a 50 mm Leica lens with a bayonet mount (i.e. apart from the Summarit, Summilux and Noctilux lenses). The red point on the intermediate piece is placed opposite the red ring on the Leica CL bayonet and locked by turning it to the right. The lenses fit into the inner bayonet of the intermediate pieces. The lenses which can be depressed are not drawn out but are locked with the bayonet of the inner

Close-up equipment in combination with a Summicron 50 mm f/2 lens — image scale 1: 1.5, set up for photographing stamps (page 126).

connecting socket. In the case of the 50 mm f/2 Summicron lens which cannot be depressed, the lens head can be unscrewed. It is screwed into the bayonet mount (16508) and locked with it. When inserting it light pressure is exerted on the mount and it is locked by turning it to the right. The lens is then safely home. It can only be unlocked by pressing it slightly downwards and turning it to the left.

This equipment is useful in cases in which the focusing range can be established sufficiently accurately by means of the telescopic legs, e.g. when photographing flowers and plants in the open and also all kinds of different objects. With reproductions it is even possible to use the four telescopic legs as a stand. Care must be taken to make sure that the legs do not cast any shadows. (it is best to use two side lamps). When photographing in sunlight it is as well to unscrew the leg which casts the shadow: the focusing limit can still be recognized with sufficient accuracy even with three legs.

If this equipment is used in libraries and no special lamps are available for illuminating the entire surface of a copy uniformly then one can work near the window even in normal daylight. The legs are prevented from casting shadows by placing bright cards on three sides of them. If one has a ball-and-socket joint at one's disposal, it can be used to stablize the three legs. The leg nearest the time-regulating knob is unscrewed and the ball-and-socket joint is screwed into the tripod socket on the bottom cover. The copy then has to be turned so as not to cast a shadow. It is advisable to stop down the lens to f/11 and to use a cable release. When reproducing dark, glossy, copies reflections may occur. They can be avoided by placing dark cards between the rods.

The screw thread construction of this apparatus (BOOWU) can be used if an intermediate bayonet ring (14097, 14098, 14099) is inserted in the Leica CL camera. All the 50 mm lenses of Leica screw mount construction are suitable.

Special care must be taken to see that the BOOWU accessory is adjusted parallel to the lower edge of the camera. Should a correction be necessary, then loosen the three small grub screws which hold the chromium ring which improve the position: the three screws are then screwed up again tightly.

CLOSE-UP APPARATUS FOR IMAGE SCALES OF 1:3, 1:2, 1:1.5, 1:1 (no longer in production) (16511 BEEON)

This apparatus can be recommended for photographing small objects such as coins, stamps, reproductions, etc. It consists of a base, a column with a plate at the top which can be adjusted upwards and on to which the focusing magnifier or the Leica camera can be fixed in turn, also two intermediate rings for various image scales, three loading diaphragms and an intermediate bayonet ring. All the 50 mm Leica lenses can be used.

The distance (approximate) are given on the back of the tripod column. The following formats are obtained with the following intermediate rings.

Format	Image scale	Intermediate ring
72 x 108 mm.	1:3	A
48 x 72 mm.	1:2	A & B
36 x 54 mm.	1: 1.5	A & C
24 x 36 mm.	1:1	A & D

The base of the stand frames an image area of 1:3. For the other scales the area is reduced by means of inserting masks.

The illumination used for taking photographs of coins should show up in relief. The best way is to use side lighting which strikes the coin at glancing incidence and also to illuminate it slightly from the reverse side. The coin has been placed on a glass plate with its four corners supported by small blocks. Because of the distance, the edge of the coin is free from shadows.

The magnifying lens is first adjusted to suit the user's eye. The eyepiece is lowered from the highest point until the black ring on the ground glass screen comes sharply into focus. Not until then do we move the fine adjustment on the column upwards and observe the sharpness of the image on the ground glass screen. Stop 4 is useful for sharp focusing and f/11 for taking the photograph. The multiplication factor for the exposure can be neglected since the measurement is made through the lens. It is only when the exposures exceed ½ sec that reciprocity failure plays a part when taking colour photographs. The Leica CL camera cannot be placed in position until the bayonet intermediate ring is situated above on the plate support.

Visoflex I and II

In the Leica system there are various mirror-reflex adapters called "Visoflex" for use with longer focal lengths and for close-up work. Visoflex I and II have not been manufactured for some years. Visoflex I and the Leica CL camera form a very useful combination. This adapter has been specially constructed for taking photographs using a tripod. A magnifying lens is used to focus and observe the image on a large, bright, ground glass screen. The change over from a vertical to a horizontal format is done by loosening a locking device at the side and turning the camera about the transverse axis. At the same time the shutter under the matt glass screen is also turned by means of a gear wheel transmission. The housing is 63.5 mm. high and focusing at infinity is possible with focal lengths of from at least 125 mm.

Before exposing, the mirror must be swung out of the light path. This is done by means of a twin release which has two cables of different lengths. The one with the small black ring is first released and is screwed to the knob for moving the mirror. The knob possesses a milled ring which, after a slight turn, holds fast the miror which has swung out. This facilitates exposure measurement with the Leica CL camera. The small black ring on the ground glass screen is used as a guide for the field measured. The thread model of the Visolex I is utilised by means of one of the intermediate bayonet rings (14097, 14098, 14099).

The Visoflex II can certainly be fitted to the Leica CL camera, but it is advisable to use it only to a limited extent because the combination is complicated to handle. The standard release lever cannot be used. Either a twin cable release is employed or the mirror is taken out of the light path and the shutter is released by means of a single cable release. In both cases a tripod has to be used. The mirror must also be swung back for measuring the exposure time. The indicator of the exposure meter can be discerned more easily if the view through the viewfinder is darkened and the frosted masking window illuminated by means of an oblique white strip. To set up the Visoflex II, the magnifying lens is first drawn backwards (at the same time pressing the catch knob) and then the release lever is turned forwards (take hold of the lever on the axis and draw it outwards at the same time swinging it forwards). When attaching the Visoflex II to the Leica CL camera — with the red ring opposite the red spot — turn it to the right until it engages. Refit the magnifying lens again.

Focusing tables

The usual tables for the depth of field range and the corresonding scales on the lens mounts have been calculated to give a permissible unsharpness of 1/30 mm. This means that the image of a point may be recorded on the film as a small disc of this diameter. If the film is enlarged 5 times, then the circle of confusion will be correspondingly larger. With an enlargement of 12 x 18 cm the permissible unsharpness will then be 1/6 mm. The resolving power of the lenses and films of today has been improved. In special cases it may be important to take this improvement in performance into consideration. If we assume the permissible "unsharpness" to be 1/60 mm, then "in theory" the depth of field will be smaller, but the sharpness in this smaller area will have improved correspondingly.

The values for a circle of confusion of 1/60 mm can be read from the standard depth of field scales on the lens mount and from the tables. The circle of confusion will still be half the size (1/60 mm) if you stop down 2 stops more than the reading given on the depth of field scale of the lens: e.g. stop down to f/11 and read off the depth of focus at f/5.6.

The following tables are valid for lenses of the stated focal length. In common with all tables they have been calculated in this way and have not been arrived at from the photographic result. In practice the sharpness required of an image varies a great deal. Above all it must be observed that in many cases a correct "dosage" of unsharpness, e.g. in the background, will enhance the effect of the picture.

When a lens forms an image, the change from sharp to unsharp takes place smoothly without a sudden line of demarcation as one might gather from the numbers in a table. F/16 and still smaller apertures should only be used in exceptional cases, because with very small stops the resolving power of a lens is somewhat reduced by diffraction of the light. Only if it is more important to extend the depth of focus field than to impair the sharpness of the image slightly, should you stop down so far.

Depth of field for 40 mm lenses

Lens aperture (f/number)	Distance focused 0.8	0.9	1	1.2	1.5	2	3	5	10	∞
2	0.78 / 0.82	0.87 / 0.93	0.96 / 1.04	1.15 / 1.26	1.42 / 1.59	1.85 / 2.17	2.68 / 3.41	4.16 / 6.28	7.09 / 17.01	24.06 / ∞
2.8	0.77 / 0.83	0.86 / 0.94	0.95 / 1.05	1.13 / 1.28	1.39 / 1.63	1.80 / 2.25	2.57 / 3.61	3.89 / 6.99	6.35 / 23.65	17.20 / ∞
4	0.76 / 0.85	0.85 / 0.96	0.93 / 1.08	1.10 / 1.32	1.35 / 1.70	1.73 / 2.37	2.42 / 3.95	3.56 / 8.44	5.50 / 57.23	12.05 / ∞
5.6	0.74 / 0.87	0.83 / 0.99	0.91 / 1.12	1.07 / 1.37	1.29 / 1.79	1.64 / 2.57	2.25 / 4.53	3.19 / 11.67	4.66 / ∞	8.62 / ∞
8	0.72 / 0.90	0.80 / 1.04	0.87 / 1.17	1.02 / 1.47	1.22 / 1.95	1.53 / 2.92	2.03 / 5.80	2.77 / 27.47	3.80 / ∞	6.05 / ∞
11	0.69 / 0.95	0.76 / 1.10	0.83 / 1.26	0.96 / 1.60	1.14 / 2.20	1.40 / 3.54	1.81 / 8.97	2.37 / ∞	3.08 / ∞	4.41 / ∞
16	0.65 / 1.04	0.72 / 1.22	0.77 / 1.42	0.88 / 1.89	1.03 / 2.81	1.24 / 5.47	1.54 / ∞	1.92 / ∞	2.35 / ∞	3.04 / ∞

Depth of field for 50 mm lenses

Lens aperture (f/number)	∞	10	5	3	2	1.5	1.2	1	0.9	0.8	0.7	0.6	0.5
1.2	67.70 ∞	8.70 11.70	4.67 5.39	2.88 3.13	1.95 2.06	1.47 1.53	1.18 1.22	0.99 1.01	0.89 0.91	0.79 0.81	0.694 0.706	0.596 0.604	0.497 0.503
1.4	58.00 ∞	8.50 12.00	4.61 5.46	2.86 3.16	1.94 2.07	1.47 1.54	1.18 1.22	0.99 1.01	0.89 0.91	0.79 0.81	0.69 0.71	0.595 0.605	0.497 0.503
2	40.60 ∞	8.00 13.20	4.47 5.68	2.80 3.23	1.91 2.10	1.45 1.55	1.17 1.23	0.98 1.02	0.88 0.92	0.79 0.81	0.69 0.71	0.593 0.607	0.496 0.504
2.8	29.00 ∞	7.50 15.20	4.30 6.00	2.70 3.30	1.88 2.14	1.43 1.57	1.16 1.25	0.97 1.03	0.88 0.92	0.78 0.82	0.69 0.71	0.591 0.610	0.494 0.506
4	20.30 ∞	6.70 19.50	4.00 6.60	2.60 3.50	1.83 2.20	1.41 1.61	1.14 1.27	0.96 1.06	0.87 0.93	0.78 0.83	0.68 0.72	0.587 0.614	0.491 0.509
5.6	14.50 ∞	6.00 31.40	3.80 7.50	2.50 3.70	1.80 2.30	1.37 1.65	1.12 1.29	0.94 1.04	0.86 0.95	0.77 0.84	0.67 0.73	0.582 0.619	0.488 0.513
8	10.10 ∞	5.10 ∞	3.40 9.60	2.30 4.20	1.70 2.40	1.32 1.73	1.09 1.34	0.92 1.09	0.84 0.97	0.75 0.86	0.66 0.74	0.574 0.628	0.483 0.518
11	7.40 ∞	4.30 ∞	3.00 14.80	2.20 4.90	1.60 2.70	1.27 1.84	1.05 1.40	0.90 1.13	0.82 1.00	0.74 0.88	0.65 0.76	0.566 0.640	0.477 0.525
16	5.10 ∞	3.40 ∞	2.60 144.00	1.90 6.90	1.50 3.20	1.19 2.05	1.00 1.52	0.86 1.20	0.78 1.06	0.71 0.92	0.63 0.79	0.551 0.659	0.468 0.538
22	3.70 ∞	2.80 ∞	2.20 ∞	1.70 13.80	1.30 4.10	1.10 2.38	0.94 1.69	0.81 1.30	0.75 1.13	0.68 0.97	0.61 0.82	0.535 0.685	0.457 0.554

Distance focused

Depth of field for 90 mm lenses

Lens aperture (f/number) \ Distance focused	0.7	0.8	0.9	1	1.1	1.2	1.3	1.5	1.7	2	2.5	3	4	5	7	10	20	∞
2	0.698 0.703	0.797 0.804	0.895 0.905	0.99 1.01	1.09 1.11	1.19 1.21	1.29 1.31	1.48 1.52	1.68 1.72	1.97 2.03	2.45 2.55	2.93 3.07	3.88 4.13	4.81 5.20	6.63 7.41	9.30 10.90	17.20 23.90	121.60 ∞
2.8	0.697 0.704	0.795 0.805	0.894 0.907	0.99 1.01	1.09 1.11	1.19 1.21	1.28 1.32	1.48 1.52	1.67 1.73	1.96 2.04	2.44 2.57	2.91 3.10	3.84 4.18	4.74 5.29	6.50 7.59	9.00 11.30	16.30 25.90	86.90 ∞
4	0.695 0.705	0.793 0.807	0.89 0.91	0.99 1.01	1.08 1.12	1.18 1.22	1.28 1.32	1.47 1.53	1.66 1.74	1.94 2.06	2.41 2.60	2.87 3.14	3.77 4.26	4.64 5.42	6.30 7.90	8.60 11.90	15.10 29.60	60.80 ∞
5.6	0.69 0.71	0.79 0.81	0.89 0.91	0.98 1.02	1.08 1.12	1.17 1.23	1.27 1.33	1.46 1.54	1.65 1.76	1.92 2.08	2.38 2.64	2.82 3.20	3.68 4.38	4.51 5.61	6.10 8.30	8.20 12.90	13.80 36.70	43.40 ∞
8	0.69 0.71	0.79 0.81	0.88 0.92	0.98 1.03	1.07 1.13	1.16 1.29	1.26 1.35	1.44 1.56	1.62 1.78	1.89 2.12	2.33 2.70	2.75 3.30	3.56 4.56	4.33 5.93	5.70 9.00	7.60 14.70	12.10 57.40	30.40 ∞
11	0.69 0.71	0.78 0.82	0.87 0.93	0.97 1.04	1.06 1.14	1.15 1.25	1.24 1.36	1.42 1.59	1.60 1.82	1.85 2.17	2.27 2.78	2.67 3.43	3.42 4.82	4.10 6.40	5.40 10.10	7.00 17.90	10.60 194.00	22.10 ∞
16	0.68 0.72	0.77 0.83	0.86 0.94	0.95 1.05	1.04 1.17	1.13 1.28	1.22 1.40	1.39 1.63	1.55 1.88	1.80 2.26	2.18 2.93	2.54 3.66	3.21 5.31	3.80 7.30	4.90 12.60	6.10 28.10	8.70 ∞	15.20 ∞
22	0.67 0.73	0.76 0.84	0.85 0.96	0.94 1.07	1.02 1.19	1.11 1.31	1.19 1.44	1.35 1.69	1.51 1.96	1.73 2.38	2.08 3.14	2.40 4.00	3.00 6.10	3.50 8.80	4.40 18.20	5.30 89.40	7.20 ∞	11.00 ∞
32	0.66 0.74	0.75 0.86	0.83 0.98	0.91 1.11	0.99 1.24	1.07 1.37	1.14 1.51	1.29 1.80	1.43 2.10	1.63 2.60	1.94 3.56	2.20 4.70	2.70 8.00	3.10 13.50	3.70 67.90	4.40 ∞	5.60 ∞	7.70 ∞

Lens aperture (f/number)

Index

133

OTHER LEICA TITLES AVAILABLE FROM
HOVE CAMERA FOTO BOOKS

Reprints of Leica Catalogues

1931 Leitz General Catalogue
This is the earliest full English catalogue. 96 pages, over 50 illustrations covering rare items such as Compur Leica, Luxus gold plated Leica and the early view finders and accessories etc.

1933 Leitz General Catalogue
This is a fully illustrated photographic dealers reference catalogue for 1933 and covers the interesting products made in the early period. A great number of which were not illustrated in the 1931 catalogue. 65 illustrations, 96 pages.

1936 Leitz General Catalogue of 140 pages
This is the fully illustrated photographic dealers reference catalogue for 1936 and gives full information and details of all the early cameras accessories and enlarger, projectors, etc. etc.

1955/8 Leitz General Catalogue
This is a fully illustrated reprint of the Photographic Dealers Catalogue for 1955/8 and covers the models If, IIf, IIIf, Ig, IIIg and Leica 72. As well as illustrating all these cameras, virtually every accessory is illustrated even down to each lenshood.

1961 Leitz General Catalogue
This is a reprint of the Photographic Dealer Catalogue covering the M1, M2 and M3 cameras, lenses and their accessories in detail. 96 pages, over 200 illustrations, size 8 x 6 inches.

Leica Instruction Books

III, IIIa, Standard and 250 — Instruction Book, 64 pages.

IIIc, IIIf and IIIg — Instruction Book, 72 pages, 120 illustrations.

M1, M2, M3, M4, MP, MD and Motor Drives — 72 pages, 140 illustrations.

Leica Close-up and Reflex Devices — Instructions covering all models of Visoflex, Bellows, Slide Copier, Copy Gauges and Close-up Attachments, 64 pages, 80 illustrations.

Leica Enthusiasts Books

The Leica Collectors Guide — An illustrated index to Leica equipment and accessories, 72 pages with approximately 400 individual illustrations, code words and descriptions.

Leica — The First Fifty Years by G. Rogliatti — An illustrated hardback book listing all the cameras made by E. Leitz, with serial number list of screw mount cameras. 136 pages, 74 illustrations.

Other Catalogues

1936 Zeiss General Catalogue — Covering Contax and accessory range, the Contaflex, all the Ikonta and the Super Ikonta series, with details and illustrations of the many interesting Zeiss products such as Mirroflex, Ikoflex, etc. 90 illustrations, 68 pages.

Mr. Lancaster's Catalogue for 1888
It is both a catalogue of his photographic products and a manual on photography, obviously with his own equipment in mind. It gives full information on the various cameras he made, and then it goes in to details of the actual photography and processing. 96 pages, 47 illustrations.